# Genre Explained

# Genre Explained

Frequently Asked Questions
and Answers about
Genre-Based Instruction

Christine M. Tardy,
Nigel A. Caplan,
and Ann M. Johns

University of Michigan Press
Ann Arbor

Published in the United States of America by the
University of Michigan Press
Manufactured in the United States of America

Printed on acid-free paper

First published March 2023

ISBN 978-0-472-03934-0 (print)
ISBN 978-0-472-22121-9 (e-book)

2026    2025    2024    2023            4    3    2    1

# *Acknowledgments*

This project began years ago as the three of us discussed the need for more teacher-friendly resources on genre-based instruction. We are grateful to the many teachers and students who, over the years, have informed our thinking on genre and writing instruction, leading to this project. Their challenges in writing for multiple classes and disciplines or in teaching students across various educational settings have helped us understand the challenges, rewards, and importance of genre-based instruction and have pushed us to find ways to discuss pedagogy in accessible and relevant ways.

We would also like to thank Kelly Sippell, who helped us launch this project and supported our less-than-conventional approach to the book; Katie LaPlant and everyone at the University of Michigan Press, who have continued to support the project despite our pandemic- and life-related delays; and Dana Ferris, for her generous foreword. We are also grateful to two anonymous peer reviewers and to our colleagues Analeigh Horton, Hanyu Jia, Naseh Shahri, and Wei Xu, who read earlier drafts of the book and provided valuable feedback.

# Contents

# *Foreword*

By Dana R. Ferris, University of California, Davis

Over the past few years, I have given a number of talks and workshops on the topic of genre-based instruction (GBI), have published one book chapter on the topic (Ferris & Hayes, 2019), and have supervised the production of new genre-based materials for the English for Academic Purposes program I was directing or designed such materials for my own writing students. As I have spoken about GBI with teachers and administrators whom I encounter in professional development settings, the reaction is typically in two parts. First, teachers readily acknowledge that the ubiquitous five-paragraph essay is inauthentic, formulaic, and unmotivating for students (and their teachers). Second, even when teachers are persuaded that GBI is a better option, they are unsure of how to develop courses, assignments, and materials to deliver such instruction. And this second point is where this new volume of frequently asked questions about GBI fills a critical and practical gap.

This trio of authors (Christine Tardy, Nigel Caplan, and Ann Johns) are without a doubt a highly qualified group of scholar-practitioners to create this valuable new resource. All three have authored, co-authored, or co-edited scholarly books on the topic (e.g., Caplan & Johns, 2019; Johns, 1997, 2002b; Tardy, 2009, 2016) as well as student texts and/or resources for classroom writing teachers (Caplan, 2019; Caplan & Johns, 2022; Tardy, 2019a). They have taught classes for L2 students in a wide range of academic institutions and trained teachers around the world on GBI. To use Malcolm Gladwell's terminology, all three have devoted their 10,000 hours to becoming experts on GBI, and it is from this repository of expertise that the volume's 40 frequently asked questions are posed and answered.

# What the Book Covers

Well ... everything. The authors asked and answered every question I have ever heard from teachers and could have come up with myself, as well as topics that wouldn't have occurred to me, such as how to persuade faculty in the disciplines and administrators of the value and necessity of the GBI approach (Questions 38-39) or how to help students deploy multilingual resources in a GBI classroom (Question 33). In this volume, teachers have the following information and more at their fingertips:

- Introductory concepts, such as the definition of *genre* and the critical distinction between genre knowledge and genre awareness (Questions 1 and 8)

- Distinctions between GBI and traditional approaches to teaching writing (the five-paragraph essay, rhetorical modes such as compare and contrast, templates, argument, essays, research papers) (Questions 4-7, 31-32)

- How to design GBI curriculum, syllabus, and assignments (Questions 19-22) and how to find/select materials, including multimodal exemplars (Questions 35-36)

- Classroom lesson sequences using GBI, both in general and on specific subtopics such as rhetorical moves analysis, grammar, vocabulary, coherence, cohesion, register, and stance (Questions 12-18)

- Approaches to assessment of genre-based writing, including how/whether to incorporate corrective feedback (Questions 24-26)

- How to help students apply GBI to other contexts through metacognition and strategies for genre analysis beyond the writing class (Questions 27-28), through critical analysis of genres (Question 29), and through multimodal and/or multilingual assignments (Questions 33 and 36).

All of these important subtopics are presented in small, digestible chunks of information, written in clear and appealing terms, and replete with practical examples to help readers visualize whatever point the authors are making.

The authors suggest in their introduction that this volume can be used as a companion to Caplan and Johns's new student textbook, *Essential Actions for Academic Writing* (University of Michigan Press, 2022), but even if instructors find that particular text not to be the best fit for a specific group of students, the information in this volume is generalizable enough to be used anywhere, as the authors themselves note in their response to Question 30 ("Is genre-based writing instruction only for advanced students?"). As already noted, this volume is so readable and practical that teachers who are in the process of designing a course or assignment, selecting materials, or generating a rubric for assessing a genre-based task can pick it up at multiple moments and find a quick answer to their questions. I came away from reading this book with new ideas for my next writing class and grateful that the authors made the effort to share their prodigious expertise with other teachers interested in GBI. It is a welcome and timely contribution.

# Introduction

Genre-based instruction (GBI) offers teachers and students a different way to think about writing and writing classrooms. It moves us away from the teaching of prescriptive forms like templates, rhetorical modes, five-paragraph essays, and "research papers" and instead turns attention to writing as dynamic, situated, goal-oriented, and responsive to readers and communities.

But teachers have questions—and they are absolutely right to ask them. What are genres? What is genre-based instruction? What do students write if they don't write essays? Isn't it easier to teach and learn five-paragraph essays? What's the role of language in genre-based teaching? How do I assess genre-based assignments? And many more. These questions are all important, and we too have struggled with them as teachers, teacher educators, researchers, administrators, and material developers. These are also the questions we've been asked at conferences, during workshops, and in the faculty lounge.

We firmly believe that there needs to be a sea change in the teaching of academic writing, especially but not only for multilingual writers, starting with rejection of the five-paragraph essay and its attendant approach to writing as unsituated, universal, and uninteresting (see Caplan & Johns, 2019, for more extensive discussion). Genre-based writing instruction offers teachers an alternative to teaching tired and artificial forms and instead focuses on developing rhetorically flexible writers. However, we are also aware that GBI is new to many of our colleagues in all sorts of teaching contexts and that its reliance on a somewhat complex knowledge of genre and how to teach it can pose challenges to teachers (Mapes et al., 2020; Tardy et al., 2022; Worden, 2019). Unfortunately, there is also a lack of practical teacher-oriented resources to demystify and explain what genre-based writing is and how it can be implemented. This book is our attempt to offer such a resource.

*Genre Explained* presents accessible, research-grounded answers to 40 frequently asked questions about GBI. It is intended as an introduction to GBI and as a reference for current and future teachers who have some familiarity with genre approaches but want to know more. We imagine this book to be especially useful for teachers of writing in higher education, including preparation programs such as intensive English programs, pathway programs, and bridge programs. These teachers may be experienced writing instructors who are new to genre approaches, or they may be novice teachers, including lecturers and graduate student teachers. Our primary focus is on supporting writers who use English as an additional language, but the book is also very relevant to teachers of "mainstream" writing in post-secondary contexts, where linguistic diversity is also the norm. Additionally, this book may have relevance to teachers of languages other than English or to those who work in elementary and secondary contexts, but this is not the book's primary focus.

In just 40 questions and answers, our text cannot address *every* aspect of genre-based instruction, nor is that our goal. Similarly, this book is not a repository of genre-based activities or assignment sheets to be readily imported into classes. Rather, we hope to offer a grounding in genre-based instruction's definitions, principles, and practices, so that teachers can build familiarity in these areas and have tools for implementing GBI into their own classrooms in ways that are contextually appropriate. The book can be read as a companion to the writing textbook *Essential Actions for Academic Writing* (Caplan & Johns, 2022), providing the rationale behind pedagogical decisions embodied in that text. As well, *Genre Explained* would be an ideal resource for teacher preparation or support courses, such as TA practicums, MA TESL courses, or teacher orientation programs. We also hope that teachers may find the book to offer a good source for discussion in teacher collaboratives, teacher reading groups, or other professional development activities. The book pairs well with other teacher-oriented overviews of GBI (e.g., Caplan & Johns, 2019; Cheng, 2018; Hyon, 2018; Tardy, 2019a); toward this aim, we offer an annotated bibliography of additional resources in Question 40.

Taking teachers' queries as a starting point, we have organized the book around questions rather than more traditional chapters.

The answers to each question aim to be as practical as possible while also sharing references for readers who may want to learn more. The questions are clustered into five parts. Questions in *Part A: Understanding Genre-Based Instruction* probe the construct of genre and some of the terms that can be confused with genre. *Part B: Introducing Genre-Based Instruction* moves to the principles that underlie GBI. In this section, we also answer questions about how certain areas of writing (such as cohesion and coherence) can be addressed in GBI. *Part C: Designing a Genre-Based Course* addresses questions related to practices for developing and implementing genre-based curricula. In this section, we share numerous tools that can guide you in making pedagogical choices that will be appropriate in your own specialized contexts. In *Part D: Addressing Common Concerns,* we respond to questions that often arise for teachers who want to use a genre approach but are unsure how it affects their choices for assignments or how it addresses some of their other writing-related goals. We conclude in *Part E: Moving Forward with Genre-Based Instruction* by offering some tools for talking about genre-based instruction with colleagues and administrators and for learning more about genre-based pedagogy.

We make no assumptions that the book will be read in a linear manner. Instead, we imagine (and hope!) that you will use the table of contents to identify questions that are of interest to you and will dip in and out of different questions and parts of the book. We have also included cross-references throughout to help direct you to different questions where relevant. We hope that this helps you follow your own paths of inquiry.

For us, this book is an outcome of years of discussion of genre and genre-based teaching with each other as well as with numerous colleagues, students, and administrators. Condensing so many ideas into a small book was a challenge that we embraced because we wanted to create a brief and accessible text that teachers would be likely to actually use. We realize that the book will not answer *all* questions that teachers have, nor will it go into great depth on the topics covered, but we hope that it offers a way to dip their proverbial feet into the pool and to start exploring how GBI may work best in their own classrooms.

# Part A

## Understanding Genre-Based Instruction

# 1 *What are genres?*

You are probably familiar with the term *genre* in reference to categories of music, film, art, or literature. Genres are categories, and in the teaching of language or writing, we use *genre* to describe categories of texts. Texts are not necessarily written products: They may be written, spoken, digital, or multimodal, but a text is a complete unit of information. By this definition, a billboard ad, wedding invitation, webpage, text message, movie, lecture, and journal article are all examples of texts.

Crucially, a genre is not a text: A genre is a classification of texts, allowing us to recognize that texts do not appear at random, nor do they exist in a vacuum. Instead, they are used to respond to situations that occur time and time again. Genres are created and shaped by the communities of people who use them; we often refer to these communities as *discourse communities*. Discourse communities are groups of people who share some social practices and accompanying use of language. Academic disciplines, teachers, politicians, and librarians are all examples of discourse communities, and each of these communities has its own collection of genres that members use to communicate as they accomplish various actions.

We easily recognize texts when they belong to familiar genres. For instance, we can usually differentiate junk mail from the cable bill, news articles from editorials, commercials from TV programs; similarly, a teacher can easily distinguish lesson plans from syllabi. At the same time, we tacitly recognize that some genres include a greater variety of texts than others. Swales (1990) refers to "prototypical" examples of genres, with a prototype being the most typical example of a category: a sparrow is a prototypical bird; a four-door sedan is a prototypical car; a flat-ish circle of baked dough with cheese and tomato sauce is a prototypical pizza. So too in genre theory, you can readily call to mind a prototypical novel (250–300 pages of prose divided into chapters), academic journal article (10,000 words with predictable use of fonts, headings, references, figures, and tables), or wedding invitation ("we request the pleasure of your company to celebrate . . . "). However, in many genres, we can also stretch those boundaries and identify non-typical instances that, although different from the prototype, still reach the same social goals while bending the expectations for content, structure, or language choices. Sandra Cisneros's *The House on Mango Street* (1984) is a non-typical novel: It is composed of short, unnumbered vignettes, not chapters, some of which feel as though they might almost be prose poems, but it is marketed, read, and studied as a novel. Theses and dissertations have been submitted as a graphic novel (Sousanis, 2015), a rap album (Carson, 2017), and a set of films (Harris, 2010). If a student is conferred with a degree on the basis of a non-prototypical dissertation, it is still by social convention a dissertation.

Genres are not set in stone, but neither are they fleeting. In Schryer's (1993) helpful formulation, they are "stabilized-for-now." For example, although Chris, Ann, and Nigel all wrote traditional doctoral dissertations as monographs with six or seven chapters, in the sciences and some social sciences, the multi-manuscript dissertation is no longer an innovation but a requirement for many doctoral students. Meanwhile, in creative fields, multimodal dissertations are becoming increasingly common (Ravelli, Paltridge, & Starfield, 2014). In other words, genres evolve to meet changing social needs. This doesn't mean we should not teach genres, but it does mean that we cannot teach genres as fixed templates (see Q6), nor can we reject examples that don't fit neat textbook models of genres. One of the benefits of a genre-based pedagogy is that we can teach students to recognize the common features of a genre and still understand the degree to which their texts should be prototypical or can stretch or bend conventions (Tardy, 2016).

# 2  What are the differences between genre and text?

A "genre" is an abstraction. It represents a category of texts that share "family resemblances" (Swales, 1990, p. 49), certain features that appear in most of the texts in that genre category. These shared features could include:

- The typical situation/context in which the texts from the genre appear. In classrooms, textbooks, lectures, lecture notes, and multiple-choice exams may be the key genres. Courtrooms, religious institutions, stores, dormitories, and newspapers have their own sets of genres.
- The purpose for writing, that is, the writer's goal. In addition to attaining a grade, goals could be to persuade, instruct, request, critique, explain, or define.
- Predictable, but not completely fixed, patterns of development. Request emails, research papers, and newspaper editorials all have their own typical sequence of information, from which some writers will sometimes deviate.
- Certain types of specialized language, layout, or conventions.
- A "register" (see Q14) that is generally adopted by writers of effective texts in this genre.

A text, on the other hand, is a single item that is written, spoken, or multimodal. If a text writer successfully employs the "family resemblances" of a genre, it then might then become what Swales (1990) called a "genre exemplar," a realization of the genre that is produced in that particular text for a specific rhetorical situation.

This distinction between genre and text becomes clear in a genre-based curriculum. In curricula of this type, students are exposed to a variety of genres: pedagogical, disciplinary, professional, or everyday (see Q3). Students compare, contrast, and then write individual realizations (texts) from a genre. By understanding both the constraints upon a specific genre and the possibilities for variation and innovation (see Tardy, 2016), students can learn to write specifically and effectively for each new situation.

# 3 What are some genres that students commonly encounter?

Within different contexts, we can distinguish among three broad kinds of genres (Johns, 1997):

- *"Homely"* or *everyday genres* (Miller, 1984) are those we use to engage in the social contexts of our daily lives outside of the classroom. Students will likely be familiar with many kinds of everyday genres, including various types and functions of social media posts, text messages, and service encounters, as well as wedding invitations, shopping lists, and internet ads. This familiarity can be useful when introducing the concept of genre.

- *Pedagogical genres* are those that only exist in and for education. Created for the purposes of teaching and/ or assessment, these vary considerably among academic disciplines and may even be unique to a single instructor or classroom (Melzer, 2014). Pedagogical genres include examination prompts, mathematical problems, short-answer questions, and certain types of library research papers. For example, a pedagogical genre, the case write-up, was developed by business schools to teach fundamental management principles and is sometimes used to assess students' knowledge and analytical skills (Forman & Rymer, 1999). At the graduate level, the thesis or dissertation is "the ultimate school paper, the final school-based display of knowledge and ability" (Paré, Starke-Meyerring & McAlpine, 2009).

- *Disciplinary and professional genres* are embedded in the work completed in academic disciplines, professions, or other discourse communities (see Q1). Professional genres are context specific even if they are given similar names.

For example, a "report" means something quite different to an educator, a policy analyst, a radiographer, or a police officer. Disciplinary genres, which can also vary in a number of ways, include journal articles (that is, empirical research papers), medical notes, budgets, or proposals.

It would be misleading to consider only everyday, disciplinary, and professional genres to be authentic, since this would imply that pedagogical genres are inauthentic. Within a course with certain objectives for students, pedagogical genres are definitely authentic because, for the most part, they have purposes, contexts, writers, and audiences. They are usually graded and may even serve as gatekeepers for advancement. Classrooms are real social contexts; instructors are real audiences; and students need to see themselves as real writers as they respond to classroom assignments. Meaningful assignments, whether in everyday, pedagogical, or disciplinary genres, should be appropriate to the class context in which they are situated, encourage students' agency as writers, engage them in the work, and focus on skills, abilities, and understandings that are transferable to other writing situations (Eodice et al., 2017).

# 4  Is the five-paragraph essay a genre?

The five-paragraph essay is sometimes described as a pedagogical genre (a genre used solely in the context of classrooms; see Q3). However, we believe the five-paragraph essay is best referred to as a template, not a genre (see Q6).

It is worth emphasizing that not all texts with five paragraphs are five-paragraph essays, nor do all five-paragraph essays have exactly five paragraphs, although they nearly always do in writing textbooks. Instead, the five-paragraph essay is best understood as an approach to writing that reduces all texts to a single, unvarying template, consisting of an introduction with a "hook" and "thesis statement," identically structured paragraphs with "topic sentences" and "concluding sentences," and a conclusion that reiterates everything that has preceded it (Caplan & Johns, 2019). In essence, the five-paragraph essay is the outcome of a mindset that prioritizes form over function, structure over meaning, and predictability over variation.

The rigidness of the five-paragraph essay form stands in stark contrast to the flexibility of actual genres. For example, consider the everyday genre of the restaurant menu. Menus tend to have fairly recognizable forms: They all include the available dishes, and most include prices. Many are organized in a predictable way, beginning with early parts of the meal (such as appetizers) and moving through to the main dishes, possibly desserts, and finally drinks. There are plenty of variations, though, depending on the type of cuisine, the formality of the restaurant, the different meals being served (e.g., breakfast vs. dinner), and how many items the restaurant sells. Common features or conventions of the genre (such as the listing of food items with optional descriptions and prices) help readers recognize a text as a menu, but menu writers still have a great deal of flexibility in what content they include, how they arrange it, and of course how they design it visually.

The five-paragraph essay, in contrast, is presented to students as a rigid and static structure, as demonstrated by its very label, which dictates that text must be in paragraphs, of which there must be five. Adding or omitting a paragraph (for example, assigning a three-paragraph essay) is actually not a variation as long as the text is written with no attention to audience, purpose, or context. This is very different from writing an effective op-ed column, film review, or business report that happens to contain five paragraphs but only because the content, setting, and goals led the writer to choose this length and organization. Genres are categorized based on their shared goals, contexts, activities, or actions (Miller, 1984; Rose & Martin, 2012; Swales, 1990) and not only their form (see Q1). The recognizable form of a genre is the *result* of writers repeatedly responding in similar ways to a similar situation. This repeated use leads to what Swales (1990) has called "family resemblances"—that is, common (though not necessarily *required*) elements in texts or their contexts (see Q1 and Q2).

# 5 What are the differences between a genre and a mode?

In many second-language writing and composition textbooks, the table of contents looks like this: *the narrative essay, the descriptive essay, the compare/contrast essay, the argument essay* (etc.). The distinguishing features of each chapter—description, narration, comparison, argument, and so on—are known as discourse modes. Modes are ways of organizing information, but they are not the same as genres. That is, we don't see "the compare/contrast essay" as a genre.

Genres are categories of texts that all respond in more or less similar ways to the same situation (see Q1, Q2). Genres evolve to fit the needs of their users in a particular context: a grant proposal, a request email, and a classified ad look different because the people who write and read them have different needs. As such, genres change over time as needs and contexts themselves change: The scientific research paper of today is reminiscent of but not identical to the early *Philosophical Transactions of the Royal Society* (Bazerman, 1988). By contrast, modes are static and formulaic. They are presented as unchanging patterns of discourse, hence the definite articles in *the* compare/contrast essay and *the* descriptive paragraph. As Miller explained, modes present "a completely situationless, audienceless, approach to writing" (Dryer, 2015). For example, outside a writing classroom, no-one talks about writing "a compare/contrast essay," and the only reason for writing one is precisely in order to practice a certain type of writing. The assumption that such tasks will prepare students for complex assignments that involve some aspect of comparison seems optimistic at best.

Some of the modes are also vast: In just one corpus of student writing, for instance, Nesi and Gardner (2012) identified six unique types of argumentation, which are used in response to different prompts and situations. In other words, there is no such thing as a single "argumentative essay." Instead, there are expositions, discussions, challenges, commentaries, critiques, and more. While some arguments may have a thesis and three sub-points, this formulaic strategy cannot be applied to every task that calls for argumentation. Thus, teaching the modes as if they are uncontroversial and universal can set students up for failure.

Another problem with modes is that they are often seen as universally applicable to any type of writing. However, we know that genres vary widely according to the academic discipline or other discourse communities (see Q1) to which they contribute. An argument in history is not the same as an argument in biology: It has different structure, use of evidence, expectations, and conventions. Therefore, rather than learning modes, students need to learn how to analyze the *actions* they are expected to take in a particular writing task and consider how those actions are influenced by context and discipline. In other words, modes have some value because students do have to describe, compare, contrast, and argue things in their writing, but teaching through genres enables them to learn how to put these modes into action effectively in different ways in different genres. When the modes are replaced by actions, it is easier to see how different *genres* take up actions. The methods section of a lab report *explains* what the researcher did just as the manual for a flat-packed bookcase *explains* how to assemble it. However, the level of detail, use of technical language, relation between text and images, format, and purpose of the texts are very different.

One way to teach a genre-based course even within the scope of a mode-based curriculum is to identify genres that are relevant to your students' needs and that enact the modes you are told to teach. For example, instead of asking students to compare and contrast themselves and their best friend, you can ask them to compare two competing products, websites, apps, services, restaurants, or stores in an email to you or a blog post. Rather than argument essays, students can write op-ed columns, letters to the editor, fundraising letters, or persuasive articles for a school magazine. At the very least, you can contextualize their arguments by having them explore argumentation in a particular discipline. Other examples of both pedagogical and everyday genres in which one action or mode predominates can be found in *Essential Actions* (Caplan & Johns, 2022).

# 6 What are the differences between a genre and a template?

One of the criticisms that has been leveled at genre-based writing pedagogy is that it simply replaces one set of templates (such as the five-paragraph essay) with another. While there is certainly good and bad genre-based teaching, there is nothing about a genre approach that requires form-based templates for any writing tasks (Hyland, 2004). In fact, it is important to help students see that genres are not synonymous with templates.

Templates are relatively detailed guides for producing some kind of product (e.g., a woodwork project or a PowerPoint presentation). At best, templates provide a structure, organization, and design details; the writer simply needs to individualize the content. Many word processing programs provide templates for common types of writing such as recipes, newsletters, menus, or résumés. Generally, the elements provided by the template (visuals, font type and size, text areas) cannot be altered, or at least not significantly. Instead, the writer works within the constraints of the template.

In essence, templates can lend support for writing within a genre, but templates are *not* genres themselves. Genres are categories that include common ways to respond to a particular situation (Q1). Any given genre category includes a range of texts, some with strong similarities but also some with variations, even, at times, extreme variations. Therefore, templates could be of some initial use for some genres, but of less use for other, more variable genres. For example, when purchasing a home in the United States, sometimes (if a house is in high demand and has numerous potential buyers) buyers will write a short note to the owners hoping to persuade the owners to sell to them rather than someone else. A friend of Chris's recently bought a home and went through this process, but rather than writing a note, he and his wife, young child, and baby recorded a short video explaining why they loved the home.

The owners watched the video over 30 times and then sold the home to the young family. Clearly, the family deviated from a typical approach to this genre, but in this case their unconventionality was very effective! Had they simply used a template, introducing themselves and saying why they loved the home in a short letter, they may not have been so lucky.

Templates aren't necessarily always bad. In fact, some genres have such tight conventions that they demand template-like responses. Tax forms or medical intake forms are extreme examples; in academic contexts, grant proposals also tend to follow fairly rigid rules about formatting, structure, and even content. In addition, templates can be useful for introducing students to new genres. Lab report templates, for example, can be very helpful. Rather than see the choice to use templates as a yes/no binary, it is worth looking at the extent to which any given genre is more rigid or more flexible (Tardy, 2016) and also considering the way that the template may be used in instruction.

For example, many instructors teach students to write an annotated bibliography as part of the process of writing a research paper. It makes sense to provide a fairly strict annotated bibliography template to ensure that students engage in the activities that are most useful for their research, such as:

1.  The use of a consistent documentation style.
2.  A summary of the main ideas of the article in 2-3 sentences and in their own words (to demonstrate comprehension)
3.  1-2 sentences explaining how and where writers will use the source in their paper (to teach the important skill of choosing sources that are relevant to the task)
4.  A sentence evaluating the reliability of the source and addressing any potential inaccuracies or biases (to practice critical research skills, especially if using digital sources); see Caplan & Johns (2022) for more details.

On the other hand, personal statements are highly flexible in their structure, register, and contents, as befits a genre whose purpose is to demonstrate the writer's individuality. In fact, admissions committees readily recognize and may penalize formulaic or templated statements in students' personal statements.

The scientific research paper or journal article is a good example of a genre that appears to have a rigid template but in fact allows considerable variation depending on the field (Cheng, 2018). Although the Introduction–Methods–Results–Discussion (IMRD) structure is very common, it is far from universal, even in the physical sciences where the format originated (Swales & Feak, 2012). For example, Cheng (2018) found that journal articles in physics and mathematics rarely follow the IMRD structure. Meanwhile in some journals that publish basic scientific research, the methods section appears at the end of the article, only in the online but not the print version, and/or in a tiny font (e.g., *Molecular Cell, Nature, Journal of Clinical Investigation*). This format is known as Introduction–Results–Discussion–Methods (IRDM) and requires a very different approach to writing both the methods section, which is less prominent, and the results, which are foregrounded:

> Because the methods are listed at the end of the paper, or online, the reader is not exposed to details of the experimental protocols and methods before the results are presented. Therefore, the rationale for why these experiments were performed, how they were performed, and how the data were analyzed has to be presented in the Results section to pull the story back together for the reader. (Derrish & Annesley, 2010, p. 1226)

Even the introduction section in a research paper turns out to be quite variable. Although Swales's (1990) widely taught Create a Research Space (CARS) model with its three-part move structure accurately describes many journal articles, it does not account for all introductions in all journals (Samraj, 2004).

This leaves the teacher with at least two choices:

1. Have students read and write conventional texts in the target genre that follow the expected move structure, such as CARS or IMRD for a journal article, or situation-problem-solution-evaluation for a case study or library research paper. At the

same time, students should be made aware that they are writing in this way for the pedagogical purpose of learning about the prototypical structure of texts in this genre but that they should interrogate their future assignments (or journal's submission guidelines) for variations.

2.  Invite students to collect several examples of texts in the target genre in their field of study or on a particular topic. Although this works especially well for graduate students learning how to write research papers or grant proposals (Cheng, 2018), undergraduate and high school students can also be taught to conduct genre analyses at their own levels of comprehension. (Q10 and Q12 explain in more detail how to do this.)

The same approach can be taken with less complex or academic genres where the uncritical adoption of a template would hide underlying variation, such as recipe blogs or request emails. By teaching students to make informed choices rather than unquestioningly follow a template (including the five-paragraph essay; see Q4), you are starting to teach genre awareness, which will serve them now and in the future (see Q8).

# 7 What are the differences between genre and argument?

There are at least two common misunderstandings about argumentation that have been perpetuated by mass-market textbooks and in online teaching advice. Perhaps the most common misunderstanding is the belief that everything's (simply) an argument, as a popular textbook by Lunsford & Ruskiewicz (2012) attests. In fact, university assignments are often more complicated by other actions than students may realize. For example, Pessoa and Mitchell (2019), in their study of a business (information systems) course, found that though an argument was required in an assigned text, it was to be preceded in student drafts by both description and analysis. A second misunderstanding relates to a default structure evidenced in the "argument essay," a typical pedagogical genre in ESL and First-Year Composition (FYC) textbooks and classrooms (see Q4). In most five-paragraph essays based principally upon form, the claim, often referred to as a "thesis," appears at the end of the introduction. Both of these assumptions can be difficult for students to discard from their past instruction and often lead to tenacious writing schemas, preventing novice writers from being open to argumentation in other forms or to other types of actions in texts.

In genre-based instruction, another point must also be made clear to students: Argumentation and genre are quite different. *Argumentation* is an action realized in a variety of ways in different genres. On the other hand, *genre* is a broad, abstract concept for a category of situated texts (Q1). Defined principally by communicative purpose, genre "arises from a community's need to carry out specific goals" (Tardy, 2019b, p. 28). To emphasize this point, Tardy notes that "writers 'argue' through many genres, and in any given situation, they choose the genre (or genres) that will be most effective" (p. 32).

Disciplinary, professional, and everyday genres necessarily vary depending upon their goals and how those goals are typically attained with certain audiences through texts (Q3). For instance, research argumentation in the sciences, engineering, and the social sciences often requires that the claim, suitably hedged, appear in the discussion or conclusion, only after the results have been analyzed—and certainly not at the end of the introduction, as is the case in some argument essays. A more everyday genre, such as the opinion editorial, may be organized in a problem/solution framework, with the solution, found at the end of the text, serving as the claim. In some texts where argumentation is a principal purpose, the claim is implied. In many other texts, there is no claim, present or implied, since the principal purpose is not to argue but to explain, describe, narrate, or analyze.

Students sometimes misunderstand the purpose of an assignment and the action to be taken. In a study of how source texts and writing prompts influence students' decisions about what genre to take up as they write, Miller et al. (2016) found that among undergraduate history students writing to prompts that were intended to elicit argumentation, "many students instead wrote less-valued genres . . . engaging in 'knowledge telling' rather than 'knowledge transformation'" (p. 20). The researchers note that "for reasons invisible to the professor" (p. 20), the students had surmised that the prompt and the source text were calling for knowledge-telling responses rather than for more sophisticated argumentation.

At other times, particularly in students' first years of college, a "knowledge-telling" response developed from multiple sources is required in a prompt (see Melzer, 2014). Here, for example, is one of Ann's prompts (for first-year college students) that requires *explanation* rather than argumentation:

> **Context**: *The students in a social and behavioral sciences class had been reading about the problem of chronic homelessness. They had also taken notes on presentations by experts on this topic. Realizing that viable solutions were not yet on the horizon, the instructor assigned the students this prompt, requiring them to <u>explain</u> the problem but not try to solve it through making an argument.*

**Prompt:** *Working from at least four of your sources, use headings to organize your text around topics related to chronic homelessness (e.g., housing, criminalization, lack of political will or resources), explaining why this problem seems to be intractable.*

Considering the fact that the students were familiar with the argument essay often taught in U.S. secondary schools, it is not surprising that they felt compelled to create a five-paragraph argument essay, making claims and providing evidence from sources, even though they were not encouraged by the prompt or instructor to do so. It took a considerable amount of effort on the instructor's part, in addition to students' redrafting of texts and revising of the prompt, to dissuade students from their initial plans and encourage them to write a headed, explanatory, problem-solution paper.

At least two conclusions can be drawn from this discussion of the role for argumentation in a genre-based classroom. First, teachers need to provide instructions within the prompt that make very clear both the genre and the actions to be taken. Second, when "argument" is identified by students or colleagues as a genre, we teachers need to correct them by saying: "No, it's not. Argument is one of several actions that writers can take in different ways and in multiple genres."

Often argumentation essays are analyzed and written through the lens of rhetorical appeals: ethos (engendering trust in an audience by projecting authority), logos (appealing to reasoning, building a logical argument), and pathos (appealing to audience emotions). We believe that these terms may not be the most accessible for students, and that there are less abstract ways in which these three rhetorical strategies can be accomplished through genre studies. Ethos can be discussed through using the Rhetorical Planning Wheel (see Q10) to investigate the author's stance and background as revealed by the roles they take up, the purpose of the text, and the language used. Logos is closely related to issues of coherence and cohesion (see Q16 and Q17). Pathos is seldom evident in formal academic prose; however, there are some genres, like the personal statement, that do use emotional appeals. (This genre is presented at length in Caplan & Johns [2022], Project 4.) Furthermore, superficial analyses can lead novice writers to falsely believe that ethos, logos, and pathos are simple, unitary concepts. In fact, there are many ways to establish authority, draw on the ethos of cited sources, develop ideas logically, and appeal to readers' emotions, all of which vary widely by genre. Therefore, while rhetorical analysis can be a useful and valuable writing task (see Caplan & Johns, 2022, Unit 9), it is not generally the most effective starting point for a writing course.

# 8  *What is genre knowledge?*

In the simplest terms, our genre knowledge encompasses what we know about specific genres and the concept of genre, as well as our ability to use that knowledge when writing texts within a genre category. Research over the past few decades has helped immensely in giving us a better picture of what genre knowledge actually entails. Generally, scholars now think of it as encompassing two related areas of understanding: (1) an in-depth and situated understanding of a particular genre and how it is carried out; and (2) a broad, metacognitive understanding of genre as a concept. The first area is sometimes referred to as *genre-specific knowledge* and the second as *genre awareness* (Tardy, 2019a; Tardy et al., 2020).

When we think of genre-specific knowledge, we often think about the knowledge of what texts within a genre *look like*—that is, some of the common patterns or conventions in terms of their language choices, structure, or even design. For example, when shopping online, we can usually recognize the manufacturer's description and customers' reviews, two different genres. But because genres are really forms of social practice (that is, ways of getting things done within discourse communities), they require much more than recognition of the surface features of a text. Tardy (2009) outlines four dimensions of genre-specific knowledge that characterize what experts know about a genre: knowledge of rhetorical features (e.g., the kinds of evidence needed, ways to appeal to an intended audience, strategies of persuasion), knowledge of subject matter (e.g., the content being communicated), knowledge of processes related to the genre (e.g., how the genre is composed, disseminated, possible mediums and modes), and knowledge of form (e.g., linguistic choices, structure, design, even mechanics). When we first encounter a genre, we may have very partial genre-specific knowledge, but with repeated engagement with texts from a genre (and its users), we can develop a more robust, multi-dimensional knowledge.

Genre knowledge also includes knowledge *about* genre—that is, a broader understanding of genre as a concept and of how genres may be analyzed in order to understand them better. This *genre awareness* is a kind of metacognitive knowledge, a "consciousness of genres' rhetorical nature and of their potential for adapting to writers' particular purposes and situations" (Devitt, 2009, p. 348). It may also include "becom[ing] more aware of the interaction between process, intertextuality, and products, and the variations among texts" (Johns, 2002a, p. 246). That is, genre awareness involves understanding how texts and genres are related to other texts genre chains and sets. For example, texts that preceded the publication of this book included a proposal, many types of emails, a contract, anonymous reviews, and colleagues' written and oral feedback; future genres related to this volume might include book reviews, social media posts, presentations, and perhaps articles and books that cite our work.

Genre awareness can also be critical, including an awareness that writers make choices to suit the needs of a given writing situation and that these choices (and, indeed, the existence of certain genres) also reflect and create certain social values and ideologies—often in ways that benefit some and exclude others (see Q29).

A question for the writing teacher, then, is whether to teach students how to write specific genres (such as lab reports, case studies, research papers, and personal statements) or to teach *about* genres so that students are equipped with the metacognitive skills to analyze and write in new genres that they will encounter. In some contexts, the genres students need to produce are very limited and may therefore be the sole focus of instruction. However, in most writing classes, we simply do not know what types of writing our students will need to do outside our own syllabus. Fortunately, research suggests that classroom instruction can support the development of genre awareness and genre-specific knowledge, and that each can inform the other (e.g., Cheng, 2007; Negretti & McGrath, 2018). That is, genre awareness can contribute to our knowledge of specific genres, and genre-specific knowledge can also expand our broader genre awareness. An important implication for teachers is that instruction should aim to develop *both* genre awareness and genre-specific knowledge, though the emphasis may be more on one area than the other depending on student needs and educational context.

# Part B

# Introducing Genre-Based Instruction

# 9 What is genre-based instruction?

Genre-based instruction is an approach to teaching that aims to build students' understanding of how writing responds to particular contexts, situations, and needs through genres. This approach also helps students learn how to produce specific genres that are important to them now or will be in the future. In other words, genre-based instruction aims to develop students' genre knowledge (see Q8), including their understanding of how genres work, how genres can be analyzed, and how specific texts within a genre are successfully carried out (through language and rhetoric). Through such knowledge, genre-based courses strive to build writers' rhetorical flexibility, so that they can respond effectively to the many different writing situations they will encounter.

Of course, the precise goals of any given genre-based course will vary; emphasis may be paid to some aspects of genre knowledge over others depending on the learning/teaching context. For example, in a setting in which the students need to learn a specific genre or set of genres to succeed in their job or academic studies, learning about and producing those genres effectively may be a primary goal. On the other hand, in a writing course at the start of a liberal arts undergraduate degree, students will need to develop a broader toolkit of strategies, understanding how writing responds to a wide range of unique audiences and purposes.

That said, genre-based instruction is never *solely* about learning features of specific genres. Raising students' awareness of how different writing choices (related to language, structure, content, design, etc.) affect the success of a text in different situations is an essential part of genre-based teaching. Toward this goal, Swales (1990) has emphasized the value of what he calls "rhetorical consciousness-raising" tasks, which "sensitiz[e] students to rhetorical effects, and to the rhetorical structures that tend to recur in genre-specific texts" (p. 213). Through such tasks, students explore the choices available to writers for texts in specific genres, as well as the effects of those choices. (See Q9 and Q10 to learn more about rhetorical consciousness-raising tasks.)

In other words, all genre-based courses aim—at least to some degree—to equip students with analytic tools for understanding how writing works as it responds to situations and how tasks play an important role in achieving that aim. Swales (1990) defined tasks in genre-based teaching as "a set of differentiated, sequenceable goal-directed activities drawing upon a range of cognitive and communicative procedures" (p. 76) that support developing genre knowledge (see Q8). For example, students learn how to analyze lexical features (like the use of *I* or the use of technical jargon), grammatical features (such as the use of passive voice, active verbs, or sentence fragments), and rhetorical structures (how information might be sequenced within a text). They may even analyze the common practices around certain genres, like the technologies that can be used to compose a text in a genre or when and how a genre is commonly disseminated to its readers. For example, if students are analyzing grant proposals, they might interview experts to learn how long the process typically takes, who is involved, and how various collaborators might coordinate their responsibilities. Through such analyses, students gain a metalanguage for talking about texts and genres, which also supports their understanding of how writing works.

A common misconception is that genre-based writing instruction is simply about "teaching genres." But it is more accurate to say that such instruction is about teaching *about* genres and giving students tools for understanding how to approach unfamiliar writing situations with some success. In some classrooms, this may mean focusing on a few very specific genres that students need to use; but even then, genre-based teaching goes beyond simply teaching the common features of those genres. Instead, a genre-based course develops students' abilities to think about why certain features might be more common than others in a particular genre or situation, how texts within a genre might vary from one another, and how writers might make choices that serve their own goals within unique writing situations. As a result, genre-based teaching is not (or at least should not be) a prescriptive pedagogy telling students how to write certain texts but rather one focused on students' exploration of writing and its related practices so that they can make astute choices in the many writing situations they will encounter.

# 10  What is genre analysis?

Genre analysis is an approach to exploring a genre through its representative texts, and it is a central feature of genre-based classrooms. If we think of genres as rhetorical actions, genre analysis may explore any aspect of a genre that helps us understand how it accomplishes those actions, including its purpose, writer's role, audience, context, structure, language, and use of sources or evidence. Genre analysis can also help uncover what variation is possible within a genre category, including when writers might make different choices and how effective those choices might be. The goal of such analysis is raising learners' rhetorical consciousness (see Q9).

Genre analysis is about analyzing and understanding a *category*, not just a single text. Here it differs from other approaches, such as rhetorical analysis or critical discourse analysis, in which the goal may be to understand just one text. To understand how a genre works, we need to explore *multiple* examples, usually through a small set of texts that are representative in some way of the broader category. For example, a student preparing a science poster for the first time might browse the posters on display in their department's hallway or photos from a previous poster showcase at their school.

Writers often engage in a very informal genre analysis when they first write in unfamiliar genres. If you have written letters of recommendation for a student or colleague, you probably faced questions the first time you had to write one. You may have been uncertain about the genre because you had not seen many examples. You might have looked for letters that you had encountered when serving on a hiring or admissions committee, or you may have searched the internet for samples or tips for writing a good letter of recommendation. You might have even asked a colleague for advice. You probably did not carry out a detailed and systematic genre analysis, but you quite possibly made some attempt to understand the common features of the genre to be sure your letter would meet readers' expectations and carry out its goal effectively.

We encounter new genres on a regular basis, and we usually adopt some strategies of genre analysis informally as we try to figure out how to use the genre successfully.

There are many ways to analyze a genre in a classroom, but as an instructor you can generally follow these broad steps to implement genre analysis with students:

1. Decide what you (and your students) want to know about the genre.
2. Collect a small set of texts representing the genre.
3. Identify a few features or aspects of the genre students can analyze to answer your questions.
4. Explore the texts through various genre analysis tools. (We use *texts* in a very broad sense here: Texts may be oral and multimodal.)

The first step is important because it guides the rest of the process. Sometimes we, as analysts, want to understand a genre's form (that is, its linguistic features and structure); in other cases, we might just want to understand more about when the genre is used by a group of people (the audience) and how important it is to them. Genre analysis questions can cover a variety of topics.

One useful tool for deciding what you need to know about a genre is the Rhetorical Planning Wheel (RPW) (Caplan & Johns, 2022), a visual that helps students to identify important components of a genre and to figure out the role each component plays in an individual text (see Figure 1). The RPW can be used to read and analyze texts as well as to draft, peer review, and revise them. The components of successful text writing in a genre are listed around the edge of the wheel.

The RPW can help prompt specific questions that should be asked about a genre. For example:

- *Purpose*: What is the genre used to do? That is, what, in general, are the writer's purposes? What actions does the writer take in this genre?

**Figure 1.**  Rhetorical Planning Wheel (Caplan & Johns, 2022)

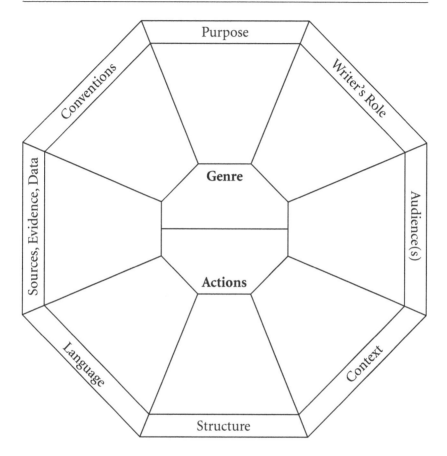

- *Writer's Role*: Who typically writes in this genre? How are writers granted "legitimacy" in this role? What is their relationship to readers?
- *Audience(s)*: Who typically reads in this genre? If there are multiple audiences, who are they and how might their backgrounds and goals align or contradict?
- *Context*: In what context is this genre typically produced, distributed, and read? What are some important or unique aspects of this context?

- *Structure*: How is content typically structured in texts of this genre? Why are texts often structured in this way? What are some structural variations?

- *Language*: What are some typical features of texts in this genre, for example, related to vocabulary, sentence structure, and grammar? What do these linguistic features help writers accomplish?

- *Sources, Evidence, Data*: What content is typically included (and not included) in this genre? What kinds of sources (if any) are used, and how are they attributed? What kind of evidence is most (or least) persuasive? If data are used, how are they presented?

- *Conventions*: What features help readers immediately identify a text from a particular genre (e.g., paragraphing, headings, terms of address)?

Once you have a sense of what you and your students want to understand about your target genre, collect some samples. You will first want to decide how narrow or broad you want your collection to be. Consider the genre of a brochure, for example. Brochures make up a very broad category, which could include organizations' brochures, product brochures, or service brochures. All are informational and promotional texts, but they may differ somewhat. Depending on your teaching goals, you may want to include different kinds of brochures or just focus on one kind. As another example, if students were analyzing abstracts, they would want to consider the different kinds of abstracts that exist (for example, conference paper abstracts, grant proposal abstracts, research article abstracts) and whether they want to focus on one sub-category or compare a few different ones. They should also consider whether they want to understand abstracts in one discipline or perhaps across two or more disciplines. These goals will affect the choice of text samples to collect.

With your sample texts collected, you are ready to design genre analysis activities for your students. Throughout this book, we describe some of the common tools and approaches for helping your students analyze genres, such as analyzing audience and context (Q11), rhetorical moves (Q12), and language (Q13-15, Q18).

We want to emphasize that genre analysis and genre-based pedagogies are *inductive* forms of learning. Instead of teaching students about a genre and then looking at examples that illustrate those features, students themselves come to conclusions about the genre through their own guided explorations. This approach allows them to develop their familiarity with tools of analysis, which they may also use outside of the classroom when encountering new genres. Genre analysis can also help to "destabilize" (Johns, 2002a) students' preconceived ideas about writing, deepening their understanding of how texts and writers respond to unique writing situations. Asking students to explore variation within genres is also important so that they can start to see that genres are not templates but instead that each text within a genre responds to its unique situation and that—in many genres—writers have some room for individual expression (Tardy, 2016, 2019a).

# 11 What are the roles of audience and context in genre-based instruction?

In genre-based curricula, students don't just write; they write *something* for *someone* for some *purpose*, in a specified *context* (Tardy, 2019a, pp. 16–17). Both audience and context play key roles in genre-based instruction because a text composed for one situation is often not appropriate to another, even if it is from the same genre and driven by the same purpose. To take a simple example, the features of a menu at McDonald's would not be appropriate for a menu at a fancy sit-down restaurant because of the difference in context. Similarly, a résumé that is appropriate for one job may need to be revised to fully address a new employer audience and position.

When faced with a writing task, students should attempt to determine as much as they can about the audience and the context as they draft their text. One typical audience in a classroom is the instructor. This individual's values, goals, and preferences can be studied through the class syllabus, lectures, an internet search, the writing prompt itself, or a rubric, if one exists. By examining the course syllabus or listening to the lectures, students can identify the central concepts or arguments that will be the focus of an assignment and how they might be discussed in a paper. Another audience, more broadly, might be those in the disciplinary area of study. Students who have already selected a major field of study can investigate the genres of the discourse communities in their major to gain more insight into disciplinary audiences. An additional more direct and personalized way to investigate the immediate audience and context is for students to visit the instructor, particularly with drafts of the assigned paper, and request an evaluation of what they have written, listening carefully to what the instructor comments on or notices. It is also useful for students to request a model student text response to the assignment, asking the instructor to go through the model showing why it meets the task requirements.

Student writers should also try to understand the writing context as closely as possible. For pedagogical genres, the context is often the classroom or lab; in this case, audience and context may merge and can be considered together. However, if a non-classroom audience is specified (e.g., the school newspaper, an employer, or readers of a blog), the writer would be wise to study what is published in the designated platform or publication. What roles do writers take in this publication? What publishing specifications can be discovered? What is the register employed? Do the writers need to sound like students or experts? What information do writers need to include to inform readers? What does the audience already know that can be left out?

The importance of audience and context in genre-based instruction cannot be overemphasized. Writers who carefully research these components considerably improve their chances for successfully producing a text.

# 12  *What is rhetorical moves analysis?*

Moves analysis is a particular kind of genre analysis that aims to understand a genre in terms of its rhetorical "parts," also called "rhetorical moves" (or simply, moves). Moves are, essentially, the components of a genre that carry out a particular rhetorical function (Swales, 1990); in the Rhetorical Planning Wheel (see Q10), moves relate to the genre structure. Texts within a genre tend to use similar (though not identical) patterns of moves, so it can be very helpful for students to learn how to identify these patterns and their variations.

Moves can be difficult to understand without examples, so we'll start with a brief illustration. Chris received the following emails from students who requested an extension for an assignment in her course:

*Email #1:*
Dear Professor Tardy,
Is it possible to request a small extension on the Class Observation paper? I have 4 assignments due at the same time and there are literally just not enough hours in the day to accomplish everything.
Best,
[Student]

*Email #2:*
Dear Dr. Tardy,
I hope this email finds you well. I regret to inform you that due to my poor time management I will be unable to complete the Student Feedback Assignment by the start of class today. I humbly request an extension until midnight tonight in order to complete the assignment. I am more than willing to accept whatever penalty you see fit.
Regards,
[Student]

*Email #3:*

Hi Dr. Tardy,

Can I get an extension on the article annotations? I'm running out of time . . .

Thank you,

[Student]

As you can see, there is variation across these emails, but each includes one key (and required) move, which we might call *request an extension*. That move is underlined in the emails above. This move can be considered obligatory because it is needed in order to carry out the key action of the genre. For example, emails that just related the students' busy lives and competing demands for time would fail to enact this genre effectively since they would lack the key move and would therefore be descriptions or complaints rather than requests.

The emails above include other similar moves as well, which we might label *greet the instructor* and *provide an explanation*. Although all three of these emails include these moves, some extension requests omit them (as we can attest!). Some moves, like these, can help to make the genre's action more successful. Of course, these are also cultural conventions whose absence could (inadvertently) signal rudeness, lack of respect, or entitlement. In some cultures, moves like *inquire after the reader's family and well-being* may be culturally expected, but they could seem unduly personal in most North American university contexts. Similarly, different educational institutions may have their own cultural conventions for preferred moves.

Emails #1 and #3 above are very brief, but Email #2 includes some additional moves, which we might label *open the communication politely* ("I hope this email finds you well") and *accept responsibility* ("I am more than willing to accept any penalty you see fit."). If we had a larger collection of samples, we would probably find more examples of these moves, because in our experience they appear to be fairly common.

Identifying required and optional moves can be very helpful when writing in unfamiliar genres. To help students learn to recognize moves, you might start with a short and familiar genre, like these "extension request emails." Be sure to include a good set of texts that includes some variation—you might just need a few samples for some texts, or you can collect five or more for very short texts like emails. You can start by asking students to identify any "family resemblances" (Swales, 1990) across texts and then underline or circle those. Students will also see that moves do not look identical in all texts because writers have options for vocabulary and grammar. One writer may carry out a move in a few words, while another may use a few sentences.

After identifying required or obligatory moves, students can work together to identify common but not required moves, as well as infrequent moves. (See related activities in Unit 1 of *Essential Actions* [Caplan & Johns, 2022].) It is also crucial to discuss with students *why* these moves are obligatory or common: What do they help writers accomplish? Would the use of a *provide an explanation* move make Emails #1 and #3 any more successful? How does the sequence of moves affect a text's relative success?

Once students have identified the range of common moves in the genre, they can also look for patterns in how the moves are arranged or sequenced. What is the most common organization of moves, and what are some variations that they see?

Moves can be explored through many different types of classroom activities. Students might, for example, order the sample emails from most to least successful and then discuss how the author's use of moves contributes to the success of their emails. You can also give students an extension request email in which the moves are cut up into pieces, and then ask the students to try to reassemble the moves into the most effective order (see Swales, 1990). You could give them incomplete emails, and ask them to compose any missing moves. Finally, you can engage students in questions of writer, audience, and context, discussing how choices of moves might depend on the identity that the writer wants to project, their relationship with the reader, the timing of the email request, or even how big of a request is being made (is it an extension for a homework task or a major course project?).

In short, moves analysis can provide a powerful approach to exploring how the contents and structure of texts help writers to carry out their goals.

# 13  *What does grammar mean in genre-based writing?*

*Grammar* is a shorthand for a lot of different teaching and writing practices, which may be why it has acquired something of a bad name in certain areas of the literacy and composition fields. Certainly, if grammar means naming parts of speech or completing worksheets with sentences taken out of any reasonable context, it has no place in genre-based writing pedagogy. But grammar is much more: It is the systems we use to make meaning through language, and since genre-based pedagogy is always focused on how to make the right meaning in the right context, grammar—viewed more broadly as "knowledge about language" (Rose & Martin, 2012)—should be at the heart of writing instruction.

We have to distinguish, though, between three aspects of language use, all of which play a role: accuracy, range, and register.

- *Accuracy* is synonymous with grammar for many writing teachers, and indeed there are situations where the ability to write in standardized English is highly valued and deviations are risky, such as a job application or CV. However, grammatical accuracy is not in itself the primary goal of genre-based writing instruction: After all, texts can be syntactically flawless but highly ineffective in context. Meanwhile, award-winning research papers in engineering have been found to contain numerous instances of "non-canonical" language use, a rather quaint euphemism for grammatical errors (Johns, 1993; Rozycky & Johnson, 2013).

- *Range* refers to the language resources available to the writer and may include vocabulary, grammatical structures, and collocations (patterns of words that tend to occur together). Expanding students' range of language should be an explicit goal of the writing classroom. For example, it is difficult to write effectively about multiple sources without a range of reporting verbs (Liardét & Black, 2019) or to interpret and report data without different ways of expressing numbers and hedging claims (Caplan & Johns, 2022; Swales & Feak, 2012).

- *Register*: More important in many ways than either accuracy or range is enhancing students' understanding of register. Register refers to the choices of language conditioned by the context. Understanding register allows writers to choose language that is effective for meeting the goals of the genre. Register is often simplified to *high* and *low*, but in fact it has far more nuanced variations that encompass much of what is sometimes called *style* or *voice*. For example, the choices of technical vocabulary, sentence structures, pronouns, modal verbs, and citation practices that we use in this book are different from the ways we might write an article for a specialist journal, a conference abstract, a grant proposal, or a promotion dossier, even though all of these could reasonably be called "academic writing." For each genre, it is important to understand the register choices that are available (see Q14).

Therefore, the role of grammar in genre-based writing teaching should be to enable students to select an effective register for the target genre, which may involve expanding their range of language while also paying attention to accuracy.

# 14 What is register?

Register is often described as the *level* of language, from *high* or *formal* (academic and professional writing) to *low* or *informal* (everyday and personal writing). However, this simple definition hides the value of the concept: There is no single register of academic writing but rather a range of language choices that writers make in response to the specific rhetorical situation, that is, the audience, their role as a writer, the context, and conventions of the genre (see Q10).

We can better understand register not as a single dimension but rather as the combination of three related variables known as *field, tenor,* and *mode* (Halliday, 1993):

- *Field* refers to language used to express and develop ideas: What types of nouns (concrete or abstract?) and verbs (action, linking, or reporting?) are used in this genre? What level of technicality is appropriate or expected? How are adverbs and prepositional phrases used (e.g., to indicate time, place, manner, or frequency)? What verb tenses are effective? What kinds of conjunctions and connectors are used, and why? For example, in the request emails analyzed in Q12, the field would be the topic of the course, so the writer can use shared terms such as *the next assignment* or *our presentation*. Logical connectors to express reason would be expected (*because, since, due to*) so that the writer can explain the request, and prepositions or adverbs of time will occur (*today, later, soon, on Wednesday, this week*).

- *Tenor* refers to language used for interaction and engagement with the reader, and includes hedging (showing uncertainty) and boosting (showing confidence), attribution (ways of giving credit to sources), aligning and distancing (indicating agreement or disagreement with sources), pronouns (*I, we, you*), and evaluative language. In the request emails, students will need to do a lot of work here to express politeness (*please, could you, may I*), convey a reasonable request (*a little extra time*), and show confidence they can meet the new deadline. A crucial linguistic choice of tenor is whether to express the request as a question (*could you please give me a little extra time?*), a statement (*I would be grateful for an extension*), or—inappropriately—a command (*give me a few more days*).

- *Mode* refers to language used to organize and structure a text: the information structure of a sentence, nominalization, passive voice, synonyms, and other techniques for creating cohesion and coherence (see Q16 and Q17, below). For instance, it is common to provide context for the request (*I have been working on the assignment*) and then use pronoun reference (*it is taking longer than I expected*), an example of old/new information structure (*the paper* at the end of the first clause becomes the subject of the next one).

This approach to language goes far beyond vague suggestions such as the instruction to use a "formal" register or write in an "academic" style. For example, in scientific writing with multiple authors (a journal article or a group project), it may be conventional to choose "we" or to avoid personal pronouns with the passive voice, depending on the discipline or even the publication or instructor's preferences (see also Q18). Thus, there is nothing inherently more "formal" or "academic" about impersonal writing, despite the advice offered by many websites and style guides because what counts as academic writing varies so much, and thus so do the language choices that are effective in each genre.

All students need practice analyzing the register of the genres that they are learning to write, especially (but not only) English learners and multilingual students. While errors in accuracy may be fixed or excused, an inappropriate choice of register can make the writer seem rude, stuffy, or unaware of the needs of their audience. Most writing teachers can tell stories of emails they have received with unintentionally awkward register choices. Likewise, we have seen students adopt overly formal registers in settings such as discussion-board posts, where writers may be expected to communicate somewhat colloquially with peers while still showing a grasp of the content by using some technical terminology.

# 15 How can grammar, vocabulary, and writing instruction be effectively integrated?

An important task for all novice writers, especially English learners and multilingual students, is to expand their linguistic repertoires so they can effectively write in more academic and sophisticated genres (Schleppegrell, 2004). This means that vocabulary and grammar can and should be integrated in writing classes. Here are some suggestions for paying attention to language at different stages of genre-based instruction (see Q9):

- When studying examples or models, ask questions that draw students' attention to particular language choices. Verb tenses are often a good starting point, but other useful targets include pronouns, active/passive voice, nominalizations, reference words (such as *this, these,* and even *the*), and stance markers (see Q18).

- Help students connect the patterns of language to the actions, or rhetorical goals, of the texts. For example, why does the writer choose active or passive voice in describing methodology? Why is the present tense used in a review of a book that was written years ago? How does the use of nominalization help create cohesion between sentences in a textbook explanation (e.g., "water evaporates from the surface of oceans" might become "surface evaporation" in subsequent sentences)?

- Before starting a writing task, you might teach a mini-lesson on a structure that is highlighted or useful in the target genre. For example, relative clauses are frequently found in definitions (e.g., "a citation is a reference to a source *that is used in a text*"), while the present perfect tense is used to show development over time, such as when describing a graph (e.g., "the cost of childcare *has increased* dramatically").

- Joint Construction and other forms of collaborative writing (see Q21) are especially productive for language instruction since the act of co-constructing a text naturally raises questions about the words, forms, grammar, and punctuation. These brief instances of attention to form are sometimes called *language-related episodes* (Swain & Lapkin, 2002), and they have the potential to promote second-language acquisition, although they are likely to be useful for all students. During teacher-led Joint Construction, you can prompt students to attend to language with questions like: *How else can you say this that would be more effective in this genre? Can you use a nominalization here? How can you connect this sentence to the previous one? Would a different tense be better here?*

- You can ask language-focused questions during peer review and self-editing, requiring students to pay attention to language as well as content and organization. Checklists, such as the ones in Caplan and Johns' (2022) *Essential Actions*, are easy ways to guide students' attention in these activities.

- Proofreading is a skill that needs to be taught and practiced. Individualized checklists can be effective (see Q26). You can also encourage students to use your feedback, peer review, and grammar lessons to develop a list of common issues that they need to edit for, such as subject-verb agreement, punctuation, and misuse of the verb *be*. (See Ferris, 2011, for more on teaching proofreading.)

Vocabulary deserves additional attention, especially but not only when working with English learners and other multilingual students:

- Teach vocabulary in meaningful contexts: Words learned in the context of a reading or writing assignment are more likely to be taken up.

- Learners need to encounter a word several times in order to learn it, so give students the opportunity to notice new words, write definitions, write example sentences, study vocabulary, and use it in assignments and short, regular vocabulary quizzes.

- Choose words to study that are useful beyond the current task. Lists like the *Academic Word List* (Coxhead, 2000) may be helpful, although studying the lists themselves out of context is unlikely to be productive. Many of the words in these lists, while more frequent in academic writing than other registers, are still infrequent overall and thus "may involve considerable learning effort with little return" (Hyland & Tse, 2007, p. 236).

- Just because a "family" of words exists (e.g., *analyze, analysis, analytic, analyzer,* etc.) doesn't mean they are all worth learning. Some dictionaries and corpora show the relative frequency of family members, and less frequent words might not be important to learn.

- Field-specific vocabulary and terminology are vital for all student writers, but they also need to learn how and when to use technical words. The decision of whether to teach technical vocabulary depends on the context. Disciplinary vocabulary may be better learned in disciplinary classes than in a general English or writing class. On the other hand, if all the students in an ESL or writing class are preparing for studies in the same or similar field, then integrating discipline-specific vocabulary will be relevant, authentic, and motivating.

Another especially important part of vocabulary is what are often called *lexical bundles*. Lexical bundles (also sometimes called *fixed phrases, formulaic phrases,* or *collocational sequences*) are groups of two-, three-, four-, or five-word collocations that "follow each other more frequently than by chance" (Hyland, 2008, p. 5). Lexical bundles are more than off-the-shelf packages of vocabulary; they help construct the meanings of texts in specific genres. For example, in course syllabi, frequent lexical bundles include *during my office hours* and *our goal is to*, but in university course catalogs, common lexical bundles are *in the college of* or *from the office of* (Biber & Barbieri, 2007).

Not surprisingly, the use of lexical bundles not only varies across genres but also sometimes across disciplinary uses of the same genre. For example, Hyland (2008) found that some lexical bundles—such as *on the other hand, in the case of, as well as the, these results suggest that*—occurred frequently in published articles and theses across disciplines. However, science and engineering writers made more use of lexical bundles related to research procedures (*the operation of the, the use of*), quantification (*the wide range of the, the magnitude of the*), or description (*the structure of the, the surface of the*), while writers in fields like applied linguistics made more use of lexical bundles that helped orient readers to the text itself (*in the case of, with respect to the*). While these examples are specific to certain kinds of writing in certain disciplines, they illustrate that lexical bundles are an important feature of genres, both in terms of their conventionality *and* variation. In a genre-based classroom, teachers can draw students' attention to the role that lexical bundles play in genres, and students can begin to build their repertoires of lexical bundles to use strategically in their writing.

Lexical bundles that recur across multiple disciplines can be found in the *Academic Formula List* (Simpson-Vlach & Ellis, 2010), the *Oxford Phrasal Academic Lexicon* (https://www.oxfordlearnersdictionaries.com/us/wordlists/opal), and the very helpful *Academic Phrasebank* (https://www.phrasebank.manchester.ac.uk/). Subject-specific phrases can be identified using simple corpus searches or personal corpora (Caplan, 2019; Charles, 2014).

We think it is useful for writing teachers to think of vocabulary and grammar as two sides of the linguistic coin: Grammar structures need to be taught with their attendant vocabulary (e.g., reporting verbs, conjunctions, prepositional phrases), while vocabulary needs to be taught with its grammatical properties and patterns (e.g., count or noncount noun, transitive or intransitive verb). Together, these aspects of language provide students with valuable tools for expressing their ideas. While it is important to encourage students to draw on their existing language(s) so that their writing accurately reflects their individual voices, it would be a disservice not to also take the opportunity of the writing classroom to teach students new ways of expressing themselves, especially when this opens up access to high-stakes genres.

# 16  How can I teach coherence
   in genre-based instruction?

One of the frequent rationales for using the five-paragraph essay and other templates for writing is the claim that these formats give students a structure without which their writing would devolve into an incoherent jumble (see Q4). But in genre-based pedagogy, students can learn to write coherent texts without a heavy reliance upon rigid templates. Instead, they can examine how coherence is maintained within the genres they are studying, thus recognizing that texts are constructed in different ways for a variety of different audiences and purposes. Coherence refers to the unity of the entire text, the logical flow of ideas, but as with all aspects of genre, the nature of a coherent text depends on its purpose, context, and audience. For instance, press releases conventionally start with the most important discovery, event, or prediction and then build the background. Readers—usually journalists and editors—expect an inverted pyramid structure. Reading quickly, they will initially find the most important information. The details are found later in the text, which ends with the author or institution's contact information (see Caplan & Johns, 2022, Unit 4).

Devoting instructional time to issues of coherence is particularly useful when teaching academic genres, because English tends to be considered *writer-responsible* by experts in intercultural communication (Hinds, 1987; Qi & Liu, 2007). That is, in contrast to texts in some other languages, non-fiction texts in English should be relatively easy for the reader to follow because proficient writers take on the responsibility for *leading the reader through,* overtly showing the relationships between ideas and providing explicit definitions and background information. In some other academic cultures and languages, texts are considered to be *reader-responsible*: The reader is responsible for mentally assembling the argument and context from clues provided by the writer, who prefers to avoid patronizing the reader with background they already presumably know.

If readers and writers are familiar with a genre (that is, if they are members of a discourse community that uses this genre), they will already have knowledge about how texts are typically organized and what actions the writers tend to take within these texts (see Q8). For these individuals, then, a well-written text is situated, coherent, and organized appropriately for the genre. However, students are often assigned to write in texts from genres that are unfamiliar to them. In this case, they can be assisted in using genre analysis (Q10) to determine how the components of successful texts are integrated to achieve coherence in their assigned genre. Through genre-based curricula, units, and lessons, students develop this sense of coherence as they become analysts of new genres and eventually members of new discourse communities. If, for example, résumé genres are new to them, they can compare and contrast two sample texts—a résumé for a job as a company manager and a curriculum vitae for an academic position—noticing how the two examples are the same or different and considering what makes each appropriate and coherent for its particular audiences and contexts.

One important way that coherence, and thus "writer responsibility," can be taught is through the principle of rhetorical *moves* (Swales, 1990) (see Q12). A move is a functional section of text that is required or optional, fixed or flexible, in a particular genre. Many disciplinary and professional genres require a number of moves, organizing the complete text to achieve the writer's goals (see Q12). It should be pointed out, however, that viewing a text as a series of moves is not the same as following a text template. Moves are genre specific: Most research papers, for example, are not written with the same moves as reports and résumés. Second, texts in genres are typified by both family resemblances *and* variation (Q1, Q2). Writers need to be aware of how moves in their assigned texts resemble or are different from other texts in a genre and study the choices writers make depending on their academic discipline, topic, purpose, audience, and context.

And there can be considerable variation! Personal statements, for example, which have few basic moves in common, vary considerably depending on a number of factors such as the audience and the prompt. Sometimes, these texts are quite personal, beginning with an anecdote related to the writer's life and pursuing a theme that demonstrates the writer's motivation or ability to succeed or change. Other examples are more academic, intended to demonstrate the writer's knowledge of the "ways of being" of a particular discipline. Both are personal in that they focus on the writer; however, the organization and focus of the moves are quite different.

Swales (1990) points out that moves in introductions differ as well, depending upon academic discipline, context, and other factors. In one text, the writer may summarize the key findings at the end of the introduction, while in other texts, this practice would not be acceptable. Some introductions announce the structure of what is to follow; in others, structure is not mentioned.

Because the job of an academic writer is to lead the reader through the text (at least in some genres and languages), writers often use metadiscourse to tell the reader how a move will be organized. The author might begin a section of text with:

- "Part I of this review traces the development of the process."
- "A list of these difficulties will be presented and discussed below starting with xxx and ending with yyy."

Sometimes, writers use metadiscourse to introduce a topic that follows:

- "The negative aspects of this methodology will be taken up next."
- "Another problem that needs to be resolved focuses on the use of this type of engine."

In other cases, writers may announce their purpose:

- "My purpose here is to explain xxx methodology."
- "The intent here is to demonstrate why this earlier theory is rather weak."

Other than using metadiscourse in framing sentences, writers can achieve coherence through the use of visuals (e.g., charts and graphs) or bulleted sections. Whatever the case, the expert writer follows the conventions of the genre and employs metadiscourse effectively, thus contributing to a text's coherence.

How can we teach coherence? We need to use multiple sample texts from the genre to be assigned, selecting specific items for students to notice. Here are a few possibilities for *coherence* activities:

1.  Ask students to examine a full text, perhaps one in the sciences, that includes headings, visuals, and formulae. Tell them to identify what features of the text help readers to process and understand the information presented. Analyze how these features are introduced and discussed in the text.

2.  Assign moves analysis (Q12) of a single section type from two texts in the same genre (e.g., the Results sections of two research papers or the request move from two student-teacher emails). Ask students to discuss how these moves are the same or different both structurally and linguistically. Why do they think this is the case?

3.  Ask students to identify the framing sentences and the metadiscourse for different sections of one or two texts from the same genre. They should notice, in particular, what each framing sentence does. Does it state the writer's purpose? Indicate how the next section will be organized? Focus on the topic of the next section? A combination of these actions?

# 17 How can I teach cohesion in genre-based instruction?

In contrast to *coherence,* which refers to enhancing the comprehension of complete texts or large sections within them, *cohesion* refers to the devices that maintain meaningful relationships between and across sentences (Halliday & Hasan, 1976). Effective cohesive devices lead readers from sentence to sentence, increasing reader understanding of where each sentence is going and what it is doing. Not surprisingly, how cohesion is achieved will vary from genre to genre and sometimes from text to text within a genre.

Many writing textbooks present cohesive devices as lists of transitional words organized in broad functional categories. Certainly, these words and phrases are crucial to reader understanding, but they have different meanings and appear in different genres written in different registers (see Polio, 2019, for a critique of this "lists" approach). Like the genres in which they are found, cohesive devices are situated; their choice can vary according to context, structure, purposes, and register (Q14) of a section of text.

Here are some of the many ways successful cohesion can be achieved, depending upon the genre and context:

- *Employing this* + a general noun: The structure *this/these* before a general noun that describes a category, such as *approach, problems, issue,* or *components,* is an effective way to create cohesion between sentences. An example: "Swales introduced an approach to moves analysis in article introductions. *This* approach has become popular in genre-based classes."

- *Using information structure* to guide the reader: The first part of a sentence is considered to be the *Theme,* and is usually the place for old or familiar information, with new information in the rest of the sentence. The old information from one sentence becomes the *theme* of the next sentence, as can be seen in the opening paragraphs of this chapter: "effective cohesive devices" in the second sentence picks up from "the devices that maintain meaningful relationships" in the first sentence; "these words and phrases" in the second paragraph refer back to "lists of transitional words," and so on.

- *Using the passive voice*: One important function of the passive voice, which appears in many academic genres, is to move old information into the *theme*. This choice can ensure that key information is foregrounded and remove distracting, vague subjects (e.g., *people, we, everyone*). An example might be: "Results were verified through three different experiments."

- *Employing nominalization*: One of the most powerful cohesive applications in English involves the ability to take a verb or clause and "pack" it into a noun phrase. This is called nominalization and it helps create cohesion without repetition. Nominalization is especially common in the Theme of the sentence as a way of taking information from the previous sentences and turning it into a single noun. For example: "Reflection encourages writers *to think about their own thought processes. This metacognition* has been widely studied as a key to improving writing."

- *Inserting connectors/signposts*: According to Halliday and Hasan (1976), these "transition words," also called conjunctive adverbs or conjunctions, can be subdivided into the functions that each type serves: *additives* (*in addition, furthermore*), which connect units of language that are similar in meaning; *adversatives* (*but, however*), which do the opposite, showing contrast with what has just been written; *causals* (*therefore, because*) showing results or reasons, usually related to effects; and *temporals* (*first, at the same time*), which help readers to understand time order in a text. To be successful, writers select from these and other possibilities for use in a text from a genre. In some cases, possibilities for selection may be quite limited. When facilitating a workshop with civil engineers, for example, Ann and the participants found that in their disciplinary research genres, *however* is by far the most common connector used to signal the gap in the previous research typically found in an introduction. Here is an example of the use of this adversative leading to the gap: "*However,* work of this type is still in its infancy."

A single sentence in a text may contain multiple cohesive devices, perhaps a connector, the passive, and a nominalization. However, the use of conjunctions (*moreover, on the other hand, thus*) as connectors, the "signposts" in writing, is less frequent than many learners assume, or are taught, since these devices generally signal *major changes* in direction the text will then be taking (Hinkel, 2002).

How can cohesion be taught in genre-based instruction? These are suggestions to consider:

1.  Select one section or paragraph from a sample text your students are studying; teach the concept of Theme (or "old information" and "new information"), and ask students to underline the Theme or identify the old and new information in each sentence. Discuss with the students how the thematic structure promotes cohesion and helps readers to understand the text. Students might then write a summary of the section studied, paying particular attention to what begins the sentences in their own texts.

2.  Nominalization enables writers to present processes (usually verbs) as things (nouns). There are various ways that a nominalization can be formed (Caplan, 2019, p. 127): using a verb as a noun (*plan, increase, change*); using an *-ing* form of the verb as a gerund (*writing, teaching*); adding a suffix to a verb (*erosion, measurement*); adding a suffix to an adjective (*appropriateness, activism*); or adding a suffix to another noun (*adulthood, capitalism*). Show students samples of these

possibilities, and then ask them to find nominalizations in the sample texts they are studying. Or provide verbs and adjectives to students from their sample texts and ask students to convert these into nominalized forms.

3. In a groundbreaking article on the use of the passive voice, Tarone et al. (1981), after analyzing research articles with a disciplinary expert, found that the passive can have specific uses in research genres. In the astrophysics texts they studied, the passive was employed only for certain rhetorical functions: to discuss an established procedure (*has been employed in previous studies),* to discuss the related work of others in the same field, or to describe the writer's proposed study. Teach these possibilities and then ask students to identify passive sentences in sample research articles they are studying, hypothesizing about why the writer(s) chose to use the passive in each case.

# 18  How can I teach stance in a genre-based classroom?

Often, novice students are asked by their teachers to "express their opinions about a topic" rather than merely to inform their readers. In addition, they are told that their opinions have to be supported by evidence appropriate for the topic and the audience they are addressing, and often, that they need to use an impersonal register. Students may understandably be confounded by the apparently contradictory requirements to write impersonally but still advance an opinion or argument. The result may be "genre confusion," in which students produce a different genre than intended by the prompt. For example, they may write a narrative instead of an argument (Miller et al., 2016) because they are not aware of how language choices can allow them to take a stance toward the ideas, thus making an argument and not a simple description of events. Writers' choices are genre specific: Stance— a writer's attitude toward their content—is expressed differently in a lab report, the Results section of a history paper, and an opinion editorial. In addition, language choices revealing a writer's attitudes toward a topic, an article, an event, an experience, or the writer's audience (that is, the writer's stance), will depend upon who the writer is, the audience, and the context where the writing will be published or evaluated.

As noted earlier (Q14), one of the most frequent questions students ask is whether they can use the first-person pronoun, *I*. They are confused by the plethora of bad advice about "academic writing" in textbooks and on the internet that fails to recognize that writers engage with their readers in genre-specific ways and that, therefore, sometimes using *I* will work–and sometimes it won't. Instead of helping students to employ *I*, many writing guides tell them to always write in the third person. However, this can lead to some very strange results. Nigel assigns his students a cover letter in which they are asked to reflect on their portfolio of writing from the course. One student tried to write their letter without using *I*, leading to such awkward phrasing as: "Much was learned in this class." Clearly, first-person pronouns are available and even expected in genres where writers reflect, such as a cover letter, a personal statement, or a discussion-board post, but they are also increasingly used in empirical research papers and dissertations. Note that we have appropriately used first-person *we* throughout this book.

Here, we turn again to important terms in genre-based instruction, terms that are closely related to pronoun use. Stance and engagement are related; they are used differently by some linguists and genre scholars, but they both essentially refer to the ways that writers demonstrate confidence or doubt, take a position or remain neutral, and show support or keep a distance from claims and ideas in their text (Hyland, 2005; Martin & White, 2005). These choices are crucial for writers: They can make an argument sound too weak or arrogant, exaggerate or underestimate the importance of research findings, or push a text into an inappropriate register.

Here, for instance, are some examples (underlined) of stance choices found in a literature review that was a class assignment for undergraduates studying to be teachers, based on a taxonomy developed by Hyland (2005):

- In an underline{unusual} article by Freire, the author discussed his early education. [Unusual is an *attitude marker* in this taxonomy.]

- Perhaps this publication could be considered the most important in the field. [Perhaps is a *hedge*, showing the author's unwillingness to take a strong stand toward the status of a publication.]

- First translated from Portuguese into English by Myra Ramos in 1970, *The Pedagogy of the Oppressed* is the most important text in the study of critical pedagogy. [Most important is a *booster*, that is, a phrase that enthusiastically promotes a particular idea or author.]

- I am arguing here that there is no competition between the work by Freire and that of other critical pedagogues. [The use of *I* here is "self-mention" that positions the writer as an expert with an argument to make.]

The importance of engagement (Martin & White, 2005), particularly aligning and distancing readers, can also be seen in the choice of reporting verbs (e.g., *Tardy claims* takes a very different stance from *Tardy demonstrates*) and the way data are presented (e.g., is 45% *nearly half*, *less than half*, or *more than 4 in 10*?).

A discussion of stance can be incorporated into every stage of the genre-based classroom. When analyzing sample texts, ask students questions that draw their attention to the way the writer engages with or disengages from the reader:

- What pronouns are used (first, second, or third person)? Where and why?

- How are sources used, if at all? Do they support the writer's claims, present counter-arguments, cite examples, or show background?

- Does the writer align themselves with particular sources, theories, or positions? How do you know?

- What reporting verbs are used (e.g., *claim, state, prove*)? How do they reflect the writer's attitude toward their sources?

- Does the writer use the grammar of modality (e.g., *can, could, may, might, probably, presumably, definitely, certainly*)? What effect do these choices have on the reader?

- How are data represented? Does the writer try to highlight any numbers or make them sound important, surprising, disappointing, large, or small?

Then, during classroom Joint Construction (see Q21), you can elicit similar structures to express certainty or hesitancy, alignment or distance. Finally, resources for stance can be included in the assignment rubric so that students focus on their language choices and construct the relationship they see as most appropriate with the reader (Q25).

# Part C

# Designing a Genre-Based Course

# 19 What is the role of needs assessment in genre-based instruction?

No doubt teachers everywhere, even if they are assigned a curriculum, attempt to assess their students' needs; that's good teaching. An English for Specific Purposes (ESP) approach can be especially useful in this effort because it has formalized needs-analysis processes and is rich in its detailed discussions of the ways in which students' needs can be measured to determine the "what" and the "how" of a writing course (Flowerdew, 2013; Long, 2005). Since genre-based instruction is designed or adapted for each academic class, carefully planned needs analyses are central to curricula and lesson planning.

In ESP, the term *needs analysis*, also called *needs assessment*, covers a broad range of course-based activities that are seen as "interdependent, overlapping and cyclical" (Dudley-Evans & St. John, 1998, p. 122). Central to ESP, and thus to genre-based curriculum development, needs analyses include *target situation analyses,* as instructors decide what genres to introduce to a class and how. In *narrow-angled* courses (such as English for Engineers) developed for students who are enrolled in a major or have a similar future profession, the genres can be determined through target situation analyses, including expert interviews, surveys, genre analyses (e.g., Samraj, 2013), and observations. However, if students are in more general, *wide-angled* courses, where a number of majors are represented, the choice of genre is often not as important as preparing students to develop genre awareness (see Q8). In these courses, the genres and activities selected are those that can assist in transfer to often unpredictable academic literacy contexts.

Needs analysis might also include researching which "large cultures" and "small cultures" interact in the learning context, as a step toward selecting genres to be introduced. Connor and Ene (2019) define these terms in this way:

> Large cultures have ethnic, national, or international group features as essential components and tend to be normative and prescriptive. Small cultures, on the other hand, are non-essentialist and based on processes that relate to cohesive behaviors within social groupings [sometimes called "discourse communities."] such as the cell biology department or law practices relating to immigrants. (p. 53)

To demonstrate how these two cultural categories affect the development of curricula, we use as examples three situations in which Ann co-conducted needs and target situation analyses in collaboration with local experts. When co-developing a curriculum for Antonine University, a French-dominant university in Lebanon with narrow-angled courses (e.g., English for Mechanical Engineers, English for Accountants), Ann learned as much as possible about the country itself (the "large culture") and the professions that were most valued there. On the advice of the English program director (Eid), she interviewed business and engineering professionals, individuals from the students' "small cultures," whose expectations for English use among employees were high. Based on these large- and small-culture experiences, the researchers developed specialized, narrow-angled curricula in each major content area (Eid & Johns, 2010).

In South Africa, Ann worked closely with Makalela, the chair of the English department, and his colleagues at Limpopo University, a small culture, to develop a two-semester reading and writing curriculum for first-year students representing every university major. This work involved studying the university and its students as well as the surrounding large cultures, which were still suffering from many traces of the apartheid era (Johns & Makalela, 2011).

In another project, Ann's target-situation needs analysis for her work entitled *AVID College Readiness: Working with Sources* (2009), developed for secondary students across the United States, included a study of the institutional small culture of the AVID organization, which is dedicated to enhancing first-generation secondary students' potential for college readiness and success. She also interviewed AVID teachers from large cultures from several disciplines across the country who would be using the new curriculum in their classes.

In each of these three cases, the research evolved throughout the curriculum and lesson production processes, as Ann and her colleagues interacted with key stakeholders and observed and took notes on the small-culture contexts in which the students were enrolled. Thus, the needs analyses were ongoing, as the researcher worked with local experts to understand the schools' and universities' discourse communities (Swales, 1990), as well as teachers' expectations and assignments across the disciplines.

As we know, every class we teach is a bit different, so Ann and her colleagues devised *present situation analyses*, taking into consideration current students' "lacks" and "assets" in terms of prior knowledge, literacy tasks, or language use as well as relevant "wants": the students' interests, motivations, and goals (Flowerdew, 2013). Google Forms and other free survey tools provided ways to elicit student interests and wants in these ongoing projects.

This discussion of needs and situational analyses should suggest the complexity of providing a focused and appropriate genre-based curriculum for a specific group of students, since small and large cultures and the expectations and intentions of all stakeholders influence needs and target situation analyses. In addition, as practitioners, we teachers and curriculum designers should be perpetually involved in informal needs analyses, combining target situation analysis and present situation analysis efforts to create genre-based classes suitable for our students, because as Belcher (2006) points out:

> It is probably no exaggeration to say that needs assessment is the foundation on which all other [instructional and assessment] decisions are, or should be, made. (p. 135)

# 20  What does a genre-based curriculum look like?

Genre can be incorporated into writing instruction at four levels, so it is worth differentiating and defining them. By *curriculum*, we mean an overall program of study that guides the design of multiple courses, each of which is divided into chunks we call *units* (see Q21) that are taught in one or more lessons. We start at the macro-level with curriculum for two reasons: Readers who have influence over curriculum can positively impact writing instruction by building a genre-based curriculum, while others should be aware of how curriculum shapes courses, units, and lessons so they can make small but meaningful changes and suggestions.

Since genre is concerned with types of writing that fulfill social functions, a genre-based curriculum starts with analysis of the needs of learners in the contexts in which they currently or will write (see Q19). The results of the needs analysis—as well as practical, logistical, and institutional constraints—will determine several key decisions in curriculum planning. For example, will the curriculum teach one specific set of genres or does it need to have broader goals of preparing participants to complete genre analyses and write across a range of genres, not of all which can or will be addressed in the courses?

A further important design decision is the selection and sequence of genres across a curriculum. Many writing curricula are organized by mode (see Q5), with descriptive and narrative modes taught earlier and argumentative and analytical modes taught later. However, when viewed through a genre lens, such a sequence is hard to apply. Is the Methods section of a research paper (a description) less sophisticated and demanding than a persuasive email (an argument)? A more promising taxonomy is provided by Feez (1998), who categorizes genres along a continuum from *everyday* to *applied, theoretical,* and finally *critical.* For example, descriptions are found in newspaper articles (everyday), restaurant reviews (applied), technical reports (theoretical), and interview field notes (critical). Linguistic and rhetorical demands increase along this trajectory, so it would often make sense to start with everyday and applied genres before moving into theoretical and critical ones only if the needs analysis suggests that these are important for learners. Another approach involves a *genre chain*, in which the same information is transformed repeatedly in increasingly complex genres. One genre chain we have taught draws from the students' own academic backgrounds to create a bio-statement, a résumé, and a personal statement, all self-promoting genres.

In most educational programs, it is impractical to expose students to every genre they will need now and in the future. Some genres (such as letters of recommendation) may be occluded (Swales, 1996) and inaccessible; some may require a level of technical expertise that is beyond the scope of the writing class; or some may be idiosyncratic and unpredictable, as is often the case with undergraduate student writing (Johns, 2019; Melzer, 2014). Such curricula should incorporate opportunities for teaching and learning genre awareness alongside genre-specific knowledge (see Q8), including reflective activities that enable learners to transfer their ability to write in the curriculum's target genres to novel genres in the future (see Q27).

Finally, we encourage curriculum designers to consider genres that are meaningful for learners *now* and not only in the future. Not every writing class should be seen as merely a preparatory step toward "real" writing in other domains or areas of the curriculum. However, focusing on the present situation can be especially challenging in English for Academic Purposes (EAP) and first-year undergraduate writing courses, whose purpose is often reduced to preparing students for success in future semesters or courses or, worse, teaching inauthentic writing forms such as the five-paragraph essay as a presumed waystage to proper writing later (Caplan & Johns, 2019). Students may be motivated by the prospect of success in their future studies; however, it is more likely that they will be engaged in tasks that are meaningful to them right now (Eodice et al., 2017). Therefore, some flexibility in design should allow for engaging writing tasks, which may include:

- Personal genres such as blogs or other online diaries and personal letters;

- Genres that bridge personal and professional domains, such as bio-statements (Hyland & Tse, 2012; Tardy & Swales, 2014) and homepages (Hyland, 2011), as well as social media profiles or posts, which can promote academic work while also expanding one's personal and professional network and exerting more personal aspects of one's identity;

- Promotional and self-promotional genres, including personal statements and scholarship applications (Johns, 2019; Project 4 in Caplan & Johns, 2022), job application letters and résumés (Tardy, 2019a), letters of reference and requests for such letters, reviews and book blurbs (Project 1 in Caplan & Johns, 2022), advertisements, proposals, and reviews.

- Creative writing, which can be a research method in itself (Phillips & Kara, 2021), a fun and even revelatory transformation of an academic genre (e.g., dance your dissertation, #OverlyHonestResearchMethods; see Tardy, 2016), or even storytelling and creative writing (Maley & Peachey, 2015).

# 21 What does a genre-based unit look like?

A *unit* is a somewhat vague term used to divide a course into segments, and in a genre-based writing course it is reasonable to teach each genre as a unit (see also Q21). For instance, a course preparing students for graduate school writing might teach units on summary, data commentary, literature reviews, and application essays (personal statements). The structure of the unit depends on the time and intensity of the classes. However, there are some principles that can guide decisions in designing genre-based units:

- Genre-based writing instruction should be scaffolded so that students are building skills toward mastery. That is, they should not attempt to write their texts until they have a solid understanding of the assigned genre through all the relevant dimensions of the Rhetorical Planning Wheel (see Q10). Ideally, this analysis enables students to write better drafts: Front-loading explicit instruction reduces the need for correction and remediation later.

- Genres should be explicitly taught through interactive analysis of multiple sample texts in the target genre. That is, writing starts with reading and analysis, not with brainstorming and invention, because teachers cannot generally assume students have prior experience with the target genre.

- Since a text is not a genre (see Q2), it is important to expose learners to multiple text exemplars. Doing so helps reveal both the *family resemblances* (Swales, 1990) that enable readers recognize a genre and the degree of variation and flexibility that exists within it (Tardy, 2016).

Genre educators working in the framework of Systemic Functional Linguistics have developed a *curriculum macrogenre* (Martin, 2009), or unit plan, that works well when planning instruction. This Teaching/ Learning Cycle (TLC) (Rothery, 1996) was designed for use in middle schools but has been refined and applied at all educational levels, from first grade to graduate school (Brisk, 2018; Caplan & Farling, 2017; de Oliveira & Iddings, 2014). The term *cycle* emphasizes that the following phases of instruction should not necessarily be treated as linear: A strength of this approach is that teachers may need to cycle back to ensure that students are ready for the next step.

1. *Deconstruction*: The teacher guides students in the analysis of several sample, or "mentor," texts, interactively highlighting the typical staging or structure of the genre and language choices that help writers perform the function of each stage or move and achieve the goals of the text as a whole.

2. *Joint Construction*: This is a phase of collaborative writing. In many implementations of the TLC, the whole class constructs a text together in the target genre on a new topic while the teacher prompts, elicits, recasts, corrects, and supplies words and phrases. For example, if the class has deconstructed several product reviews, they then collaboratively write a review for a real or imaginary item, such as a coffee mug, cellphone, or umbrella (Caplan & Farling, 2017). Some practitioners have added a Collaborative Construction phase after this, especially for emerging or struggling writers, where the students work in pairs to jointly write another text; this may even end the cycle (de Oliveira et al., 2020).

3. *Independent Construction*: Now students are ready to write a text by themselves! They have analyzed samples and written one or more texts collaboratively, all of which has prepared them to produce their own text in the target genre. The familiar writing process steps of planning, drafting, revising, and editing still apply, but students are prepared for success rather than set up for failure in an unfamiliar genre.

4. *Reflection*: Some versions of the TLC include a stage in which students are encouraged to reflect on the similarities and differences between the new genre and other genres they have studied. For example, how is an explanation different from a recount? This can promote metacognition and transfer to novel genres (see Q27).

The TLC is effective because it is a front-loaded and scaffolded approach to writing instruction that treats each genre as both unique and related to other genres. The TLC also encourages a consistent and meaning-centered focus on language: Students notice the linguistic forms that are functional in each stage of the genre; they negotiate the phrasing of each sentence through collaborative writing; and finally they apply their developing language skills to their independent writing. This makes the TLC especially attractive not only in ESL, bilingual, and multilingual classrooms, but in any context where students are developing the "language of schooling" (Schleppegrell, 2004).

# 22  What is an effective genre-based assignment?

In writing instruction, we can distinguish between a *prompt* and an *assignment.* A prompt consists of the actual instructions for writing: what students are to do in their texts and how they are to do it. An assignment, on the other hand, refers to the context in which the prompt is initiated and embedded as well as the steps that students will be taking to lead up to and continue writing—that is, the writing processes. So, for example, an assignment might be based upon some research the students have completed on an assigned topic or a lecture or video that they've heard or experienced.

The *prompt* tells the student writers precisely what they should do in their papers—in other words, the instructor's expectations for the final texts. It repeats the specific name ("genre") for the paper (e.g., report, IMRD research paper, response paper, informational summary) as well as points out the writer's role, the context, and the audience. The prompt also specifies requirements: sources used, what actions the students are to take (e.g., inform, respond, summarize, argue), the length of the paper, the font size, and the conventions that apply.

Palese (2021), in her research into student-preferred writing prompts in undergraduate composition classes, reports on a number of findings to be considered as we develop prompts. First of all, students want prompts that are short and not too wordy. Palese found that when students are given shorter prompts of a page or less, they tend to devote more time to analyzing them carefully and sorting out what is important. Second, the prose in the prompt text should be clear and broken up by headings and "strategic bolding" of important words. Third, necessity/ obligation modals, like *must* and *should*, help draw students' attention to important points. To this list, we would add a fourth recommendation for any genre-based class: that a prompt include all of the relevant elements of the Rhetorical Planning Wheel (Q10).

Here is an example following these criteria from an informational summary assignment in an undergraduate composition class:

---

**Paper #1: Informational Summaries of Book Chapters: Guidelines**

*Context/sources*: You and your writing group have been studying one or more chapters from Sotomayor's memoir, *My Beloved World* (2013). Using another source, Yosso's "Whose Culture Has Capital?" (2005), you have identified in your assigned chapters the assets that Sotomayor employs as she succeeds in school and in her world.

*Purpose*: To summarize an assigned chapter from Sotomayor's memoir.

*Text name*: As a group, you will prepare for your instructor and classmates *an informational summary* (Caplan & Johns, 2022, pp. 94–98) of your assigned chapter(s), focusing in some detail upon the author's assets, that is, the cultural capital that enabled her to succeed in school or in her world.

*Audiences/register*: You have two **audiences**: your instructor, who will grade your work, and your fellow students, who will peer review your drafts. Your **register** should be sufficiently clear to be understood by members of your class but sufficiently academic to be acceptable to your instructor. The language of the final informational summary should be grammatical, written in complete sentences, and carefully revised and corrected.

*Paper structure*:

- Use a title that assists readers to identify the chapter you studied, such as "Sotomayor Chapter 10: An Informational Summary."
- Begin your paper with a framing sentence, such as "In Chapter xx, Sotomayor (2013) uses two of her most important assets, her cultural capital, to succeed in fifth grade."

- Then, divide the rest of your summary into an orderly and specific discussion of the author's cultural capital, the assets you have introduced more generally in your framing sentence.

*Other specifications:*

- You must double-space, using 12 pt. Times New Roman font.
- Your paper should be 350-500 words long.

# 23  How do I teach students to analyze assignments for other classes?

Genre-based instruction is partly designed to enhance students' transferable skills. As a result of their writing classroom activities, they should be able to take what they have practiced and learned about writing into their other academic classes and professions.

According to Melzer's (2014) extensive study of university assignments across the curriculum in the United States, there are two common undergraduate assignment types: (1) in-class, short-answer tasks integral to tests, often called *essay questions*, and (2) out-of-class, longer assignments that are sometimes vaguely named *essays* or *research papers*. Unfortunately, both types can be misunderstood by students because the texts assigned have been given quite general names or because the instructions are not clear or complete. Even some of the best prompts may not include important details or may divert students from the most important goals for writing. What can instructors do to help students understand what they are to write in any context?

For in-class tasks that are referred to as *essays*, students should be warned that in most cases, the expected response may be considerably different from essays they have written in English or composition classes. For example, the short-answer test question generally requires *only* the information requested, sometimes even in bulleted form. Successful short-answer responses often lack a "hook" or an introduction, and they may not include a wind-down or repetitive conclusion. No matter what these in-class writing tasks are labeled, students can benefit by asking instructors to share examples of short-answer test instructions employed in the past, successful students' responses, and perhaps a study guide. With these tools, students can practice responding in advance to the types of questions that will appear on their "essay" tests. Students might also discover if instructors prefer their test responses to be in paragraph or bulleted form. For example, some instructors prefer bullets because student responses can be read more quickly, often by teaching assistants who are looking for specific information.

To help students prepare for short-answer tests, writing teachers can give students practice in analyzing test prompts by providing a grid that isolates the two important elements in most short-answer questions: the action to be taken and the content to be acted upon. Here, for example, is an analysis of a question found on a marketing class exam (from Melzer, 2014, p. 104):

> Describe the major factors causing changes in food consumption (Chapters 1-4) and describe the market channel for a chosen commodity (Chapter 12).

One problem with this marketing question and many others is the variability of meaning in the term *describe*. Here, this term may refer to defining (major factors) or outlining the steps (in the market channel). Exploring these possibilities with the instructor or with a study group in advance of the test can be useful. Here is a grid that students might complete to analyze this prompt:

| What am I to do? | With what information? |
| --- | --- |
| Describe | The major factors causing changes in food consumption |
| Describe | The major market channel for a (only one) chosen commodity |

Some test questions require more than one action or include more than one topic. Here is an example from a teacher-education class:

> Discuss two reasons why high-stakes examinations are often criticized. In each case, point out what groups of stakeholders tend to be most critical.

| What am I to do? | With what information? |
| --- | --- |
| Discuss | Two reasons why high-stakes exams are criticized |
| Point out | (for each reason) what groups tend to be the most critical |

After completing the chart, students can practice writing a sample response, focusing first on a short framing sentence (e.g., "High-stakes exams have been criticized as reductive and exclusionary") and then turning immediately to what they need to do (in this case, discuss the two reasons in turn with reference to specific stakeholders in each case). (See Unit 3 in Caplan & Johns, 2022, for further examples.)

Teachers looking for authentic prompts for in-class analysis can find numerous examples in the journal *Prompt: A Journal of Academic Writing Assignments* (https://thepromptjournal.com/index.php/prompt).

# 24 How should I assess genre-based writing?

Because genres vary in their audience, purpose, structure, conventions, and language use (see Q10), approaches to assessment must be sensitive to genre. A text that is successful in one genre would likely be ineffective if presented without revision in the guise of another genre. An excellent op-ed column would make a poor research paper, while an outstanding scientific grant proposal would not get published on the editorial page. Furthermore, genres are discipline specific: A scientific argument is structured and supported differently than a historical argument (Wingate, 2012). Good writing is not universal: It is genre- and context-specific (Wardle, 2017). Therefore, assessment needs to be genre-specific too. In other words, students' writing should be evaluated based on its effectiveness in representing the target genre, not in terms of general concepts of "good" writing.

Since one of the goals of a genre-based writing course is the development of genre awareness and rhetorical flexibility (see Q8), a common approach to assessment is the use of portfolios that allow students to demonstrate their growth and agility as writers. There are many ways to implement portfolio assessment in a writing course. One common technique is to ask students to select a certain number of assignments or one example each of the key genres taught, revise the papers one last time, and submit them at the end of the course with a cover letter for evaluation. The grade for the portfolio can replace any (temporary) grades given to the original assignments.

Portfolios are attractive because they provide students opportunities for multiple rounds of feedback and revision, for showcasing a range of writing abilities, and, crucially, for reflecting on the development of their texts, their writing skills and techniques, and their ability to bring the lessons learned to future tasks. The key component of a portfolio is the reflective cover letter, usually written at the end of the course, in which students look back on their writing, evaluate their progress, and critically analyze their texts and writing processes. The letter not only encourages the development of students' metacognitive skills (see Q27), but also gives the teacher valuable insight into the students' understanding of writing and genre.

Portfolios also solve a problem with traditional grading: What does it mean to calculate a mathematical average of assignments in three or four different genres? Does the average of a summary, an op-ed column, and a research paper tell us anything about the student's writing proficiency? In a portfolio, writing is assessed more holistically and longitudinally: that is, by considering the entirety of the student's work and progress during the course.

A final option worth considering in a genre-based classroom is *ungrading* (Blum, 2020). Ungrading is more than just an alternative to assessment: It entails a radical recalibration of the purpose of teaching and learning, emphasizing feedback and learning over evaluation. Teachers can take various approaches to ungrading. In minimal grading, for example, teachers use a simplified grading system, perhaps using only two or three grading levels rather than the typical five (Elbow, 1997). In labor-based contract grading, students engage in a grading contract with teachers, in which categories of assessment are based on the labor that students put into their projects, measured through time, effort, and engagement (Inoue, 2014). For instance, a labor-based rubric might assess students on meeting assignment requirements, submitting work on time, participating in activities like peer review, and the extent of revisions made to a draft. Two important principles of ungrading include a focus on feedback *over* grading and an emphasis on the important role that student reflection, agency, and self-evaluation should play in the assessment process.

While teachers have numerous options for assessment, the emphasis in a genre-based course should be on assessment that takes into account the specificity of the focal genre (rather than assessing "general writing" competence), that utilizes assessment for learning, and that helps support the course goals (see Q25).

# 25  How do I write a genre-based rubric?

Rubrics can be a powerful tool for both assessment and feedback. However, in order to be useful, the rubric has to be more specific than the typical categories of *content, organization,* and *language.* Or, at least, the descriptors that assign scores, grades, and marks to the categories need to be keyed to the actual genre in which students are writing. For example, it does not make sense to have an organization category that expects developed paragraphs with topic sentences for an op-ed column or a request email, where paragraphs often comprise a single sentence. Those genres certainly employ paragraphing, but effective paragraphs look different from those in most expository and research writing. Thus, the criteria for evaluation must always reflect the analysis of the genre that students conducted, using for example the Rhetorical Planning Wheel (Q10) or the Teaching/Learning Cycle (Q21). Genre-based writing courses cannot use universal rubrics.

The rubric for a genre-based writing assignment should consider the following aspects of effective writing (adapted from Humphrey & Macnaught, 2016):

- The structure of the text in the context of the target genre and the intended audience (that is, its coherence);
- The development of paragraphs, moves, or phases of the text (that is, its cohesion, see Q17);
- The range and accuracy of grammar and vocabulary to produce an effective register (Q14);
- The use of language to express stance, including hedging, boosting, making claims, rebutting, and conceding, as appropriate to the genre (Q18);
- Relevant conventions such as headings, paragraphing, citation, and format.

The importance of each criterion and the way it is defined will vary from task to task such that different features of the students' writing will be highlighted and prioritized depending on the prompt and genre (Humphrey & Macnaught, 2016). For example, in an argumentative text, the language of claims, counter-arguments, and refutation is critical, while in a literature review, the ways that writers report, cite, synthesize, and evaluate research are central to the success of the text. In other words, not every evaluative criterion is equally salient in every context.

A genre-based approach can also accommodate more traditional rubrics. For example, the typical categories of *content, organization, language,* and *format* can be aligned to *genre completion, paragraph development and cohesion, register* (field, mode, and tenor; see Q14), and *conventions.* In this way, the rubric can be tailored to both the rhetorical and linguistic demands of the target genre. In addition, while accuracy of grammar and vocabulary is important in many genres and educational contexts, a genre-based rubric focuses the reader's attention on the language that is functional in the target genre and register rather than the presence and number of "errors" (see also Q26). The rubric below illustrates assessment criteria for an informal summary assignment, as described in Q22.

Rubric for an Informational Summary (Peer and Instructor Review of First Draft)

| Criteria | Approaches / Meets / Exceeds | Comments |
|---|---|---|
| The summary has a title that indicates the source and the chapter studied. | | |
| The summary begins with a framing sentence alerting the reader to the topic of the text and its organization. | | |
| The text is well organized, presenting the assets/cultural capital in logical order. | | |

| Criteria | Approaches / Meets / Exceeds | Comments |
|---|---|---|
| The writers cite the Yosso and Sotomayor texts correctly. | | |
| Cohesion is satisfactory; the writers move smoothly from sentence to sentence and from one idea to another. | | |
| Sufficient detail from the chapter(s) is presented for reader understanding. | | |
| The language of the text is academic yet accessible to students. | | |

# 26 What is the role of written corrective feedback in genre-based writing?

Many teachers and students have traditionally associated grading of written assignments with marking errors in red ink on students' papers. Certainly giving feedback on a draft is a valuable opportunity to draw students' attention to both effective and infelicitous language choices. It is true that accuracy plays a role in the success of many texts, but care must be taken not to overcorrect, discourage writers, or detract from a focus on meaning, genre, and register (Q14).

In fact, the definition of an error varies by register and genre. It would be disturbing to read an email or newspaper article without periods at the ends of paragraphs, yet punctuating text messages can make the writer sound angry or offended (McCullogh, 2019). Audience, context, and purpose all move the goalposts of correctness, such as the deliberate choice to use a non-standard variety of English or even a different language in a text, a practice known as translanguaging.

It is not even clear that academic writing always needs to be error-free, even if we could agree on a standard of correctness. In engineering, for example, award-winning published journal articles are replete with *non-canonical grammar* (Rozycki & Johnson, 2013) (such as the omission of an article). Ann studied the research proposals of two engineers writing in English as their second language and found that sentence-level errors did not play a large role in the success of their texts. As the Chinese-speaking scholar explained, "I suppose we should improve our English—but why?" (Johns, 1993). So the first job of the teacher looking to give corrective feedback is to discuss with their students the expectations of writing in this genre and the range of responses that will be acceptable (which will vary by context).

Ferris (2011) provides a comprehensive summary of research and practice in responding to errors in second-language students' writing. Ferris notes that the following principles apply to all writers, regardless of their linguistic background. However, in all cases, the writing situation affects the type and extent of feedback that is effective.

- Focus on a limited number of error types in each draft. This is more effective than covering the page with red pen (or "bleeding on my draft," in the words of one of Nigel's first writing students). For example, you might decide to target only the language features you identified as especially important for the success of the genre, such as quantifiers in a data commentary (*many respondents, a large percentage, the number of incidents*) or verb tenses in a literature review.

- After that, draw students' attention to additional *global errors* that impede comprehension of ideas in the text rather than *local errors*, which may be irritants but usually have little impact on intelligibility, such as articles (*a, an, the*) or prepositions.

- Consider giving *indirect feedback* such as error codes (*wf* for word form, *vt* for verb tense, etc.) or color-coded highlighting (yellow for clause problems, blue for verb issues, etc.). This is only worthwhile if students have the opportunity to revise their writing and try to improve the problematic words and sentences themselves.

Even better than correcting errors is reading a paper that the writer has already carefully edited. To this end, you can encourage students to develop an individualized checklist of potential stumbling blocks, informed by your feedback on previous assignments or a grammar diagnostic task. Students can then work through their checklists before submitting drafts.

It is worth stressing that this approach to *reactive* focus on form, or error correction, is only valuable if students are going to revise or edit their drafts, a decision that is also affected by the target genre. Emails may be re-read once and then sent; dissertations are revised many, many times. Corrections on final drafts have much less impact on future tasks and often serve only to satisfy the teacher's sense of linguistic correctness or to justify grades. In terms of language development, it would be better to note areas of need and address them in the context of the next relevant assignment.

# 27 What is the role of reflection in genre-based instruction?

Development of genre awareness and genre-specific knowledge are core goals of genre-based instruction, and reflection is a very helpful tool for building these. Through reflection, writers look back on their work and can consider their genre analyses, their writing processes, and their text products.

Experts talk about reflection as enhancing metacognitive development. Metacognition refers to a writer's "thinking about thinking." In reflection, writers can develop metacognitively when they *intentionally and explicitly* analyze how they think and learn (Pintrich, 2002). Thus, reflection assists writers to "consider why they made the rhetorical choices they did" (Yancey, Robertson, & Taczak, 2015, p. 78) and what choices they will make when they take on a new writing task, perhaps in a new genre or in the same genre but in a new context. Therefore, reflection opens the door for writers "to recall, reframe, and relocate knowledge and practices" (Yancey, Robertson, & Taczak, 2015, p, 79). In turn, these practices can lead to metacognitive development, enhancing transfer of learning as writers "reframe and relocate" each time they draft a text.

Students should be asked to reflect either orally or in writing in different ways throughout a genre-based class. They can reflect on a writing prompt, during genre analysis activities, through paper drafting and revision, and after written products are submitted and graded or directed to appropriate audiences. Here are some reflection questions that can be posed at different stages of the writing process (adapted in part from Colorado Department of Education, n.d.):

## Initial Reflections Based on a Prompt

- What does this prompt/task remind you of? Have you been assigned similar tasks? In what ways are they similar to (or different from) what you've been assigned in the past?

- What is the assigned genre? Where can you find examples of texts in this genre to analyze?
- What are the important words or phrases in the prompt? For example, what actions are you being asked to take?
- What else do you need to know to proceed with drafting your text?

# Reflections on Texts in the Assigned Genre

- What appear to be the *family resemblances* among texts in this genre? That is, what text-internal and text-external (contextual) features tend to recur across texts?
- How different are texts within the genre? Put another way, how much freedom do writers have to "make the text their own"? What aspects of texts in the genre are more rigid and what aspects can be played with?
- Is there any component of the Rhetorical Planning Wheel (Q10) that seems to be most important in this genre?

# Planning Time Reflections

- What's your best time in the day (or night) for writing? Do you make good use of it?
- Have the strategies you're using for drafting this assignment worked in the past? Are they working for this task?
- Do you continue to revise your plans/outlines as you learn more about what is required? What have you revised consistently?

# Reflections after the First and/or Second Draft

- Do the "parts" of the paper fit together? If so, what makes them flow? If not, what changes could you make?
- Is your word choice, spelling, syntax, and punctuation appropriate to the genre and audience?
- What, specifically, do you still need to work on?
- What are the best features of this draft? Why are they the strongest?
- What makes you proud of yourself as a writer after having completed this draft?

# Reflections on Peer Review

- Did you read your paper aloud before you submitted it for peer review? What did you discover?
- Did you listen to the readers of your draft, but resist or respond when necessary?
- What did the reviewer(s) mention that you may need to work on?
- Did you find this peer review helpful for the most part? Why or why not? What was most or least helpful?

# Reflections after Submitting the Final Paper

- What did you learn about yourself as a writer during this process?
- To what aspects of writing do you need to devote more time and effort?

- In what ways are you a better writer because you completed this assignment?
- What did you learn about the genre from which your task was assigned, or about the term *genre* in general?
- What have you learned from this assignment that you can use for other writing tasks in the future?

Beyond posing reflection questions, there are other ways to encourage students to reflect that are particularly useful in genre-based instruction. For example, Cheng (2018) suggests that as students draft or revise their final papers, they annotate their texts to show how their choices reflect the *family resemblances* of the genre they are working in or highlight intentional choices that they made in their writing (and why). Reflections can also take the form of visuals that represent the writers' (changing) knowledge of a genre (e.g., Negretti & McGrath, 2018; Wette, 2017), or reflection could be presented in the form of short videos or audio clips. Providing different options for student reflection can give variety, often appreciated by students.

# 28  How can I help students use their prior knowledge strategically in approaching a new genre?

Throughout their formal education, students encounter and must learn to use new texts. At first, unfamiliar genres may seem completely distinct from what students have learned before. However, research tells us that prior knowledge can be useful, and applied, as students approach new genres and contexts. As teachers, we can help students identify connections between familiar genres and new ones, facilitating student understanding of how their existing knowledge can serve as a resource. For example, students who have completed annotated bibliographies in a previous class may be assigned a review of the literature in one of their current courses. By focusing on the purposes and actions of these two genres, students can locate similarities and differences between the two genres.

Several factors might restrict students in seeing their prior genre experiences as relevant to new writing situations. Some might have difficulty understanding how writing carried out in different contexts and tasks (e.g., high school and university, or an undergraduate writing course and an undergraduate sociology course) could share similarities. When these students view each writing situation as distinct, they tend to have more difficulty drawing on what they already know. Other students, however, consider strategies that they can use *across* genres and spaces; focusing on adaptable strategies seems to help students draw effectively on their prior knowledge (Reiff & Bawarshi, 2011).

The goal of genre-based instruction, then, should not only be to help students think about how writing varies across spaces but also to identify ways that they can draw appropriately on their previous genre knowledge when approaching new tasks. This prior knowledge may include similar (but not identical) genres as well as strategies used for unpacking new genres. Explicit reflection could be part of this process, allowing students to articulate similarities and differences among genres (see Q27). Johns (2015) also suggests having students map out features of prior familiar genres and of new genres using a Venn diagram: features characteristic of the familiar genre, features characteristic of the new genre (based on genre analysis), and features that are *shared across* these genres. This exercise helps students see how résumés, personal statements, and bio-statements are similar and different. An explicit map like this can help students productively draw on their prior knowledge but also adapt it as needed for the new context.

# 29 How can I help students critique genres?

Most of the activities that we've shared so far focus on describing genres, their typical conventions, and their variations. In some cases, however, we may want students to go a bit further by not just describing genres but also thinking about the power structures that they exist within and even reinforce. As Paré (2002) notes, genres' ritualized nature "makes them appear normal, even inevitable" (p. 59), while in fact they are steeped in ideologies. The existence of genres, Paré observes, should lead us to ask questions such as: "For whom do they 'work'? To what end? Do they 'work' equally for all who participate in or are affected by them?" (p. 59). A typical student course evaluation form at a U.S. university, for example, may seem quite innocuous until we start to examine more intently the types of questions it asks and doesn't ask, how it is used (and not used), and whose goals it ultimately serves (hint: not usually the students'). By examining questions like Paré's, genre users can begin to reflect on the extent to which they want to adhere to a genre's conventionalized forms or perhaps subvert it—even if subtly—for their own uses.

Toward this goal, Devitt (2009) has advocated for teaching students critical genre awareness—"a conscious attention to genres and their potential influences on people and the ability to consider acting differently within genres" (p. 347). Critical genre awareness aims to help students see how genres can represent particular ways of seeing and experiencing the world. Devitt suggests that students may be best able to identify such worldviews in unfamiliar genres, but that once they have accomplished that, they should circle back to exploring more familiar genres and critiquing the perspectives and norms that they too reinforce.

What does such critique look like in the classroom? Devitt proposes a cycle in which students analyze a genre, write in that genre, critique it, and finally attempt to alter it. By moving through this cycle multiple times with different genres, we can help communicate to students that genre analysis can lead to more than reproduction of dominant norms—it can also lead to change. Tardy (2016) describes a "spiralled approach" (p. 164) that moves students cyclically through analysis and production, gradually moving toward critique. Here, students (1) analyze (the genre's purpose, users, and settings; rhetorical moves; and lexicogrammatical patterns), (2) compose a prototypical example of the genre, (3) interview expert users of the genre, (4) modify their prototypical text for a new audience or setting, (5) analyze the related genres, (6) create a text that bends or flouts conventions, (7) critique the genre, and (8) create a parody of the genre (see Tardy, 2016, p. 164).

To help students critique a genre, teachers might provide a set of guiding questions. In *Scenes for Writing*, for example Devitt et al. (2004) offer questions like the following to lead students to interrogate some of the ways in which genres position users and reflect social structures:

- What does the genre allow its users to do and what does it not allow them to do?
- Whose needs are most served by the genre? Whose needs are least served?
- Does the genre enable its users to represent themselves fully?
- Does the genre create inequalities among its users that lead to imbalances of power? (p. 161)

Tardy (2016) shares questions that can help students identify "innovation potential" (p. 150), and several of these also move students toward critical genre analysis. For example:

- How accessible is the discourse community to outsiders and newcomers? How does someone become recognized as a member of the community?

- What are the roles of the writers and readers of the genre (e.g., student-teacher, colleague-colleague)? Do they hold roughly equal or different power in the situation?
- Who has more freedom to break from conventional patterns within the genre?
- What are the risks involved in innovation for different writers of the genre?
- How heterogeneous is the community? In what ways?

Students might interrogate a range of genres with such questions, from university admission essays to the ubiquitous school-based literacy narrative essay to university webpages or even social media profiles.

While questions like these offer a great start, we find that genre production is also essential in building a more critical consciousness of a genre. Creating parodies of a genre, for example, can serve as a "powerful emancipatory device" (Swales, 2004, p. 250) for students, allowing them to take ownership over a genre while engaging closely with its conventions. Playing with genres in other ways can also raise critical consciousness. Students might compose a text in a medium that is less common in the genre, such as preparing a video film review instead of a written one; they could then reflect on how the modality of the text influences who reads or produces the text and the effects that the modality might have on the text's success. Students can prepare texts that flout certain conventions of a genre; as a class, they could judge the effectiveness of their norm-breaking texts in different environments. Finally, students could also identify genres that pose accessibility issues to certain communities and create examples of the genre that increase accessibility.

In short, there are many ways to help students view genres not as simply natural ways to accomplish goals but as practices that serve the needs of particular communities—and may not serve the needs of others. With such knowledge, students may start to develop some agency in their choices as genre users, measuring how they can use genres effectively to carry out their own goals.

# Part D

# Addressing Common Concerns

# 30 Is genre-based writing instruction only for advanced students?

One of the concerns we frequently hear from colleagues is that genres appear to be only for advanced students; and consequently, less-proficient writers should be served a plain diet of paragraphs and essays. There are at least two ways to approach this question, each based upon what *advanced* means; and in both cases, our answer is an emphatic *no*.

If *advanced* refers to age and thus only to adult or near-adult students in universities or the professions, it is certainly not the case that younger students are incapable of writing in a range of genres. There is a long history of genre research and development of pedagogical frameworks for primary and secondary schools (see, for example, Brisk, 2018; Brisk & Schleppegrell, 2021; Rose & Martin, 2012). By taking a functional approach to language and writing, teachers have found that approaches such as the Teaching/Learning Cycle (see Q21) successfully engage students of all ages and language backgrounds through analyzing, collaboratively writing, and independently producing texts in increasingly sophisticated and high-stakes genres. The WIDA Consortium provides the K-12 English language development standards and assessment for more than half of the United States, and their revised framework is an example of a functional approach to literacy across all disciplines and school grades. The approach makes visible the "key language uses" that students need to interpret and produce texts in the major "genre families" in which writers and speakers narrate, inform, explain, and argue (WIDA, 2020). In this approach, language expectations become more complex as the genres become more sophisticated, but from the very start, multilingual students are engaged in developing language use that is sensitive to its sociocultural context, enabling them to have equal access to the full range of the school curriculum. In a related development, researchers working with educators in urban and refugee settings in the United States have shown the genre-based pedagogy empowers young and struggling writers to not only master genres but also deploy them for advocacy (e.g., Accurso et al., 2021; Harman & Burke, 2020).

A second way to think about *advanced* students is in terms of language proficiency. Is genre-based writing instruction only for students who are advanced language learners? Again, the answer is *no*. In needs assessments for less-proficient learners, the curriculum developer might consider the immediate writing needs, rather than future ones, to motivate the learners and give them an immediate sense of genre. Less-proficient students can also learn to write different types of emails, descriptions, summaries, and reviews (e.g., Caplan & Farling, 2017). For adult vocational students in the early stages of language development, there are often forms or short reports that they need to complete on the job as well as CVs, technical manuals, and written customer service interactions, including email and instant messaging. If these students see the immediate value in learning to write in a genre, they will be more motivated to analyze and produce texts within genres with which they come into contact.

The pedagogical misunderstandings held by teachers and curriculum developers regarding emerging academic students are often based on the belief that students need to control essay structure before they can move on to learning other types of writing. But such essays—typically following the five-paragraph formula (Caplan & Johns, 2019)—are a dead-end for students; outside of literacy classrooms, they do not exist. Instead, all students should be learning the genres and literacy practices that will enable them to engage with ideas and content *now*, not in some presumed future class, grade, or level. Thus, genre-based writing instruction should not be an approach reserved for the advanced, whatever that term means. All students—at various ages and with different language proficiencies—can benefit.

# 31 Should I assign "essays" in genre-based instruction?

There are two major problems with using the term *essay* in the academic writing classroom. The first is that many faculty across the disciplines use this term to identify almost any text the students are assigned. This, of course, is problematic because students then have no precise ideas about what they'll be writing. Instead, they should be learning the names that experts give to genres in their disciplines and work with those names.

The second major problem relates to literacy classrooms where, in many cases, *essay* refers to the five-paragraph essay. This typical writing task is basically an empty template into which students pour different types of content. Thus, "essay" is the antithesis of *genre* because it is merely a formula, lacking a specific purpose or meaning. It is not *situated,* with all that term entails (see Q4).

There is no evidence that continuous student production of traditional essays results in genre awareness or rhetorical flexibility (Q8). Nonetheless, from all accounts, template-based essays remain the major pedagogical genre in many secondary schools and in some college writing classes as well (Ortmeier-Hooper, 2017; Scherff & Piazza, 2005). Thus, when students enroll in post-secondary institutions, their experiences with writing, particularly in their English classes, may very well be severely limited by this one pedagogical form, the "essay" (Ortmeier-Hooper, 2019; Rounsaville et al., 2008).

How a genre-based course copes with the "essay" and its history with students will depend upon the level and needs of those enrolled in particular classes. For more advanced students, teachers may be able to avoid the term *essay* altogether, as assignment choices will probably be made upon the basis of students' majors or concentrations. However, during what Johns (2019) calls the "interstices," that is, the academic years "between students' test-heavy secondary school education . . . and the later periods when students are becoming initiated into a discipline and its genres" (p. 134), choice of genre for the writing classroom can be more challenging. Students' reliance on their past essay experiences may dominate their understanding of writing, and teachers may believe that they need to use the term *essay* because students may not yet be writing in the genres of their chosen disciplines.

What should teachers do? One possibility for the interstitial population is to avoid assigning texts called *essays* altogether and organize a class around one of the following: genres that represent broad categories of purposes and/or actions (e.g., various types of argument texts), source-based texts (e.g., summaries, critiques, book or literature reviews), emails with different purposes (Yasuda, 2011), or genres from a variety of situations, such as everyday texts, disciplinary genres, and pedagogical genres (Caplan & Johns, 2022; Tardy, 2019a).

There are other possibilities, as well, particularly for students who cling to the essays from their past. Tardy (2019b, pp. 35–37) points out that writing teachers can begin instruction drawing from their students' prior knowledge of the "essay" and then assist them to repurpose this familiar text type for new situations through reorienting that knowledge. Tardy suggests the following (2019b, p. 35):

- From the Michigan Corpus of Upper-Level Student Papers (MICUSP) select an Argumentative Essay. Then select one or two disciplines to examine. Ask these questions: "Can you find examples of the strict five-paragraph essay?" "Can you find adaptations of the structure?" "If so, how is it adapted?" "If you cannot find any examples, why do you think this is?"

- Explore with students some genres for which the five-paragraph essay would not be appropriate, considering audience, purpose, and other components of the Rhetorical Planning Wheel (see Q10).

- Make clear the differences between rigid rules and templates and conventions, "common or socially preferred patterns rather than static rules" (p. 3), by contrasting the static rules of the five-paragraph essay with the conventions of another genre.

- Assign a series of three writing tasks that make use of the same content but move from Task One (write a strict five-paragraph essay) to Task Two (respond with an explanation of a short survey) to Task Three (write a formal letter to university administrators sharing your views).

One answer to this question about assigning "essays," then, is that we may need to acknowledge students' past experiences with rigidly structured texts—and then move quickly on to more genre-based, situated texts.

# 32 Should I assign "research papers" in genre-based instruction?

In his extensive research on assignments across the curriculum, Melzer (2014) found that "the research paper," sometimes called a "term paper," is one of the most-frequently occurring writing tasks in undergraduate classes. Research papers of a large variety of types are common in graduate classes, as well. However, these findings must be explored more carefully to be understood.

Melzer remarked that *research paper* and *term paper* are quite general terms; thus, it is difficult for students to know what these terms mean when they're assigned in a writing class or elsewhere. In fact, *research* means many things in different academic contexts. It can be organized and presented in a large variety of ways, as well, depending upon the instructors' academic disciplines, their goals for the paper assigned, student academic levels, and other factors. Some of the differences might be attributed to an instructor's goals for students—for example, to help them to practice writing in certain part-genres such as introductions or reviews of the literature, to assist them in evaluating sources, to initiate them more fully into the discipline, or more generally, to practice writing an empirically based paper. Whatever the case, a research paper assignment should be based upon your class needs assessment and resulting goals for students. Whatever you decide, the prompt should include in some way all of the components of the Rhetorical Planning Wheel (see Q10).

For genre-based instruction, we suggest assigning relatively short papers so that you and the students can concentrate upon specific elements in the required text. If you are asking students to complete a short paper that is integral to a longer one, you can provide considerable scaffolding for the sections that are not the focus of your assignment. In a recent IMRD paper that Ann assigned to undergraduates from a variety of majors, for example, the introduction and methodology sections were heavily scaffolded so that the novice students could focus on the data commentary in a results section (see Swales & Feak, 2012, pp. 139–181). The class could then focus attention upon text coherence and the other features of this section alone.

As you create the research paper prompt and the rubric for peer review and scoring, it is useful to consider these questions:

- Why are you assigning a research paper? How does it fit within the context of the class and the goals for students? What content and/or student objectives will be emphasized?
- What type of research paper will it be? Source-/library-based or empirical?
  - If it is source based, will students be searching for their own sources or will you be providing them, thus saving time for drafting and revising and avoiding plagiarism?
  - Will they be completing some type of literature review (Feak & Swales, 2009)? For what purpose? How should the review of the literature text be organized and how many sources will be required? We suggest a few sources rather than many.
  - If empirical, what research question(s) will they be pursuing? For what purpose? What will their goals be as researchers? What aspect or section of the research will be the major focus of their writing?
  - What skills, abilities, ideas, or content will students discover or develop as they work on this paper? If, for example, you want students to comment on the data they have collected, the purpose of a data commentary should be made explicit to students. This purpose could be one of the following: to support a point, make an argument, assess theory or common beliefs, assess the reliability of data, discuss its implications, or make recommendations (Swales & Feak, 2012, pp. 140–41).

After you have answered these questions, you will be much better able to create a prompt (Q22) and rubric (Q25) that reveal to the students precisely what they will be producing for their "research paper" and why.

# 33 How can students draw on their multilingual resources in genre-based instruction?

In L2 and multilingual writing classrooms, much of students' prior genre knowledge (see Q28) may come from experiences in their first language or other additional languages. In some cases, genres may be carried out in generally similar ways across languages. Menus are an example of a genre that is—in broad terms—fairly similar across languages (though with variations across types of restaurants). In other cases, a genre may work quite differently in one language than in another. Take, for example, a résumé or CV. While versions of this genre may exist in many languages, the content included, the typical formatting, and the kinds of language choices that are common can differ quite a lot across discourse communities. Similarly, in academic genres, we can find different preferences for argumentation and source use across discourse communities.

On first reflection, it may seem that writers are at a disadvantage when learning new genres in an additional language because they may bring with them contradictory understandings of those genres. In addition, students working across linguistic *and* educational contexts (such as international students studying abroad) may find that the genres that were common in one context are uncommon in another—that is, people may need different genre repertoires in their new context. For example, a study by Artemeva and Myles (2015) found that international multilingual writers at a Canadian university were unaccustomed to many of the academic genres that they encountered in their courses. They saw these as much more formal and structured than the genres of their prior educational experiences.

Despite these potential challenges, writers' multilingualism can and does serve as an important resource. Multilingual writers' experience of communicating *across* languages may actually promote genre awareness (see Q8), or their understanding of how genres work and might be analyzed. Multilinguals, as Gentil (2011) notes, often benefit from greater metalinguistic awareness and communicative sensitivity, both of which are valuable in developing genre knowledge. Additionally, multilinguals' genre repertoires and rhetorical strategies in other languages can be used strategically when approaching genres in *any* language (Sommer-Farias, 2020).

Given these potential benefits, it becomes important for teachers to (a) acknowledge the resources that multilingual writers bring to their writing, and (b) help students develop strategies for drawing on and adapting their broad genre knowledge across languages. One important step as a teacher is to learn more about which genres your students are already familiar with in their various languages and cultures. Beginning a class with short surveys or class discussions about their prior genre experiences can give you a better understanding of students' existing genre repertoires. That information can then be helpful when new genres are introduced. You may, for example, help students see connections and differences that might exist.

Explicit comparison of texts within one genre but across languages can also be very revealing. For example, students can be asked to compare features of a genre across two different languages (see Johns, 2015, for a similar activity). Students identify sample texts in the target genre, and then they analyze features of the texts, identifying features that are language specific in the samples and also those features that are common in the texts in both languages. As a follow up, students can reflect—in writing or discussion—on why the similarities and differences might exist. Activities like this can help build students' metacognitive awareness of genre while drawing on their full multilingual resources and learning more about how to enact a genre in a specific language. They could then produce texts in the same genre in two languages, using what they have learned from their analysis. As an illustration, Chris has carried out this activity with students, transforming a literature review paper into a blog post or fact sheet for different linguistic audiences. One student wrote a literature review on challenges international students face at U.S. universities and then chose to share this information in two blog posts: one in English for U.S. campus leaders and admissions officers, and the other in Mandarin for Chinese students considering studying in the United States. He analyzed similar types of blogs in English and Chinese, locating similarities and differences, before writing his own posts. In his reflection on the assignment, he described how he modified the content and language style to be suitable for each audience. An assignment like this allows students the opportunity to directly draw on their multilingual genre knowledge in ways that can contribute to their continued development as rhetorically flexible writers.

# 34 Do I need to be an expert in the genres I'm teaching?

One frequent criticism of genre-based instruction is that it is not possible for teachers to have sufficient insider knowledge of all the genres they may need to teach (Freedman, 1993). This criticism has also been raised against teaching English for Academic Purposes more generally (Spack, 1997). It is true that instructors cannot be expected to be familiar with all of the genres that students will encounter or will need to produce. This is especially the case in classes focusing on more specialized writing in the professions or disciplines or in courses for the workplace. An emphasis on learner-driven exploration of genres, however, puts much of the responsibility on students themselves to become genre experts. The teacher then provides practice in genre analysis as students make discoveries about the texts from genres that they have explored.

That said, teachers in genre-based instruction do have a responsibility to explore and learn genres along with their students. Cheng (2018) suggests several ways in which students and instructors together might develop their knowledge of the genres the students will be required to write. First, he emphasizes the value of interacting with actual genre users. For graduate students, this might include researchers, faculty members, or advisors in their disciplines. For undergraduates, this could include professors or advanced students in their major field of study (Johns, 1997). These experienced genre users might be interviewed, observed, or invited to visit the writing class to share their insights into the genres of their communities.

A second source of genre learning, according to Cheng (2018), comes from published research. Journals like *English for Specific Purposes, Written Communication,* and *Journal of Business and Technical Communication* often publish analyses of disciplinary and professional genres, and teachers and students can learn a great deal about genres across disciplines and settings through such articles.

Finally, Cheng (2018) discusses the value of guidebooks and handbooks on writing from different disciplines. Though such guides are often not based on empirical study of genres, they can offer many insights into the values that a disciplinary community brings to their writing practices.

Ultimately, the tools of genre analysis can be applied to any genre by students and teachers. It often comes down to asking the right questions about an unfamiliar genre. Students can interrogate the components of the Rhetorical Planning Wheel: context, audience, writers' role, purpose, structure, conventions, and the type of evidence or sources that are used (Q10). A close reading of the language of exemplar texts in the target genre can also help students and teachers decide what to focus on, especially if they can ask an expert user of the genre some of the questions, and in their responses ask experts why a particular answer is appropriate for their academic texts.

Here are some questions for the experts:

- Are claims and evidence presented as factual or contested?
- Does the text make an argument or overarching claim? If so, how do writers show opinion, evaluation, and judgement through language use?
- What are the major sections or phases of a successful text in this genre?
- How is the organization signaled to readers?
- What kinds of sources and evidence are allowed?
- How is information developed and expanded?
- How much technical vocabulary is used?
- What kinds of conjunctions, connectors and other cohesive devices are common?

Overall, it is important for teachers of genre-based writing courses to have an open mind and to be curious about the genres that their students encounter—and about different texts in the same genre, as well. It is also important to be up front with students, pointing out that no one can know everything there is to know about texts from a genre; instead, the class goal should be to learn strategies that continue to expand student genre knowledge and develop transferable analytical practices.

# 35 *How do I find and use sample texts?*

Sample texts, sometimes called *mentor texts* or *exemplars* (Swales, 1990), provide a foundation for genre-based pedagogy. It is through exploration of sample texts that students learn about genres, as they identify patterns and variations across texts written in similar and sometimes distinct contexts. You might be wondering, then, where you can find these texts to use in your classroom.

One piece of advice we have is to always be on the lookout for good samples. Create an electronic folder for saving digital texts, a print folder to save samples of print texts, and perhaps even a folder in your email account to save samples that you come across in your emails. Depending on your instructional setting, you might want to save texts from a broad repertoire of genres, or perhaps texts from different communities but within the same specific genres. In some cases, you will want to have prototypical texts that illustrate a very common instance of the genre. However, you will also want to be sure that students are exposed to variation so that they can see how writers exploit genres for their own purposes and circumstances; therefore, collect texts that display variety within a genre. It can also be quite valuable to include some texts that violate generic norms in more marked ways. These texts may be successful and innovative, or they may be considered failures. Both are useful for students to explore! It is also helpful to think about the audiences, writers, and contexts of your texts and to include a range so that students might compare texts across different rhetorical situations (Tardy, 2016).

If you are teaching academic or professional writing, it is valuable to seek samples from content faculty and professionals. When they provide texts to you, you can also ask for them to share something about the context of the text production and reception, particularly if they are discussing their own writing. You can also bring expert writers to class as guest speakers or as part of a panel to discuss their writing practices within a genre or two that you are teaching.

You can find sample texts in many places. Of course, lots of texts can be located on the internet. Online corpora can also be very useful in finding samples. One of the largest corpora is the Corpus of Contemporary American English (COCA) (https://www.english-corpora.org/coca/), which includes texts from unscripted spoken interactions, fiction, popular magazines, newspapers, and academic journals. For examples of student writing, you might search the Michigan Corpus of Upper-Level Student Papers (MICUSP) (http://micusp.elicorpora.info/), which includes highly graded papers from advanced undergraduates and graduate students at the University of Michigan.

Despite the resources available, sometimes the search for texts seems maddeningly long. Texts might contain language that is too challenging for the students, may require content knowledge that students don't yet have, or may just be too long. Sometimes, sample texts are simply uninteresting! In a discussion of this dilemma, Swales (2009) advocates for the "*occasional* invocation of [teachers'] creative powers to fill gaps in materials production" (p. 12). Teachers might adapt existing texts to make them more appropriate for the task at hand or even construct new texts that are representative of the target genre and also meet instructional requirements.

In some cases, it may make sense for students to gather their own sample texts. For example, in a class on dissertation writing or writing for publication, students would be in the best position to identify sample texts that would be useful for them to explore, though they may need some general guidance. By collecting their own texts, students develop a valuable strategy that they can return to as they encounter unfamiliar genres. A challenge can be collecting texts that are narrow enough to be representative of a particular community's writing but not so narrow that students cannot explore variation across samples. Students may also consult advisors or more experienced writers in their fields to help locate appropriate text samples, especially those that are more occluded from public access.

A final challenge with using sample texts is the tendency for students—and sometimes teachers—to treat samples as models or target texts that should be replicated. When working with texts in class, then, it is important to contextualize them and to discuss what might make them successful or unsuccessful in different contexts, when written by different writers, or when read by different readers. It is also helpful to work with a range of text samples so that students see the variation that is always present in a genre. When students repeatedly look to a range of texts to answer their questions about a genre, they will start to see how individual writers make choices so that not all successful texts are identical.

# 36 What role can emerging multimodal genres play in an academic writing class?

In many L2 writing classes there is a tendency to focus on genres that are primarily communicated through traditional alphabetic text, as opposed to those that include many visuals or even sound or animation. In general, we agree that it makes sense in L2 writing classes to focus much of our attention on traditional writing. Writing is often a gatekeeping device, it is especially challenging for multilingual students, and writing development often accompanies and may even promote language development. At the same time, we believe there is value in bringing analysis and production of multimodal genres into a genre-based writing class, including genres that may seem less relevant to academic writing.

There are several reasons why multimodal genres have a place in the L2 writing classroom. First, written communication is increasingly multimodal, including both the digitally saturated world of social media as well as emerging genres of scholarly writing such as blogs, research group websites, and video abstracts (Luzón & Pérez-Llantada, 2019). Writers need to learn to take advantage of the broad semiotic toolkit available to them for communicating meaning, including "the full panoply of color and sound, still and moving images" (Belcher, 2017, p. 81). Second—and most relevant to this book—multimodal writing offers an effective means of promoting students' genre awareness (see Q8), as they explore how communication is shaped by modes, mediums, audiences, and actions. Third, multimodal writing offers students alternative ways to express their identities in writing. For example, writers who may feel constrained by their verbal communication in their L2 may be quite adept at expressing their ideas visually (Hafner, 2015; Tardy, 2005). Fourth, multimodal writing can bring to the classroom a degree of playfulness and inventiveness, perhaps a willingness to manipulate written expression in new ways, potentially "invigorat[ing] less-than-lively institutional scenes of writing" (Belcher, 2017, p. 81).

The kinds of multimodal genres that are most appropriate to integrate into a class depend largely on the students' ages, the students' proficiency levels, the broader educational environment, and the goals of the individual course. But the possibilities abound: academic posters, video summaries or abstracts, the Three Minute Thesis® (https:// threeminutethesis.uq.edu.au/), infographics or fact sheets, brochures, and social media posts are just a few examples of multimodal genres that can be relevant and accessible.

There are many ways in which such multimodal genres might be effectively brought into a genre-based classroom. Exploring multimodal texts within a genre can be a fun and meaningful way to consider the many semiotic choices writers make when writing within a genre. Multimodal genre analysis includes analyzing choices related to images, font style and size, design layout, colors, and perhaps even animation or video elements. Such analysis can help expand students' understanding of how texts are shaped by audiences, purposes, modalities, and roles, promoting students' genre awareness. Many multimodal genres, such as video abstracts, are still emerging, so exploring them can also introduce students to the dynamic and "living" nature of genres, which often tolerate greater variation in their early stages.

Exploration and production of multimodal texts can also be paired with exploration and production of more traditional print genres, as students work to transform content from one genre into another. For example, if students have already produced a text such as an annotated bibliography or a research-based summary of an issue, they can then transform their own text into an infographic or a multimodal fact sheet. By using the same content they developed in a previous project but then "re-packaging" for a new multimodal genre, students must wrestle with questions of how audience, modality, and goals shape the writing choices they make. Through this process, genre transformation can also promote students' genre awareness (Belcher, 2017; Elola & Oskoz, 2017; Tardy, 2016).

Finally, multimodal genres can offer refreshing ways to comm-unicate content and simply to enjoy writing. At the end of a writing class, for example, students might produce listicles of 10 Things Every Student Writer Should Know or 5 Strategies for Writing a Dissertation (depending on the class). When freed up from the relatively rigid constraints of more traditional academic genres, students may find pleasure in writing—which is no small thing.

# Part E

# Moving Forward with Genre-Based Instruction

# 37  How do I encourage colleagues to adopt genre-based instruction?

You may have colleagues who are skeptical of genre-based teaching or who are interested but just don't feel comfortable making the switch from essay-based writing. If you want to encourage your colleagues to make this change in their teaching, you can start by explaining the value of a genre-based approach to writing instruction. It can help to emphasize that genre-based teaching aims to raise students' awareness about writing for different audiences and purposes and also to give them tools for flexible and adaptable writing.

If teachers are on board with this general idea—that is, if they see the value in moving beyond formulaic or essay-based writing instruction—you are halfway there! A second hurdle for many teachers is knowing where to start. You might share with colleagues just a few activities that can help to raise students' awareness about how we adapt writing for different audiences and purposes (that is, for different genres). Emphasize that genre-based writing instruction focuses on equipping students with strategies for recognizing what choices in their writing (related to organization, content, language, even formatting) might be most effective in different situations.

Teachers may also be worried about how to bring a genre approach to their classroom if they have specific institutional constraints. For example, they may be required to teach certain kinds of "essays," or they may have standardized rubrics that limit the choices that students can make in their writing. Even in more restricted curricula like these, there may be places where teachers can integrate exploration of texts from a genre perspective. For example, students can compare an assigned text (such as a descriptive essay) with a related genre (such as an ethnography), or they can transform an assigned text into a new genre and reflect on their process of doing this. These may be ungraded in-class activities if the curriculum restricts grading in certain ways. Assessment is more problematic, but a genre-based approach encourages the teacher to focus more on preparing students for success and giving feedback, withholding evaluation and grades until students are ready to produce the genre independently. To this end, teachers can develop genre-based rubrics (Q25) collaboratively with students by asking them to suggest the criteria of an effective text in the target genre. This rubric can be used for self and peer review, even if another rubric is required for grading. Sharing the genre-informed rubrics can also be a way to start a broader conversation about the assessment of writing with colleagues.

One of the biggest challenges of moving to a genre-based curriculum for many teachers is simply having the resources for designing genre-based tasks. You may want to start a collaborative teacher group for sharing such activities and pooling resources that you and your colleagues use and come across. Teacher collaboration can be motivating and can result in many creative outcomes. We have provided many resources in this book (see Q40) to help you get started, but in our experience, local collaborations are just as valuable in developing a repertoire of appropriate tasks and activities.

# 38  How do I talk about genre
   with faculty across the disciplines?

Often we hear from faculty that "students can't write" or that "writing programs are not doing their job." However, there may be reasons for disappointing student papers that the faculty have not considered. One reason that should now be clear to readers of this volume is that there is a considerable variety among assignments on university campuses. In 1985, a famous compositionist, David Bartholomae, noted that "each time a student sits down to write for us [in the university], he [*sic*] has to invent the university for the occasion . . . [for example] he must work within fields where the rules governing presentation of examples or the development of an argument are both distinct, *and even to the professional, mysterious*" (italics ours, Bartholomae, 1985, p. 134). In many cases, then, the problem is not that students can't write *at all*, but that they may be unfamiliar with the ways different faculty want their texts to be written.

How can faculty in the disciplines make their assignments less mysterious, perhaps to themselves as well as to the students? How can writing requirements become more visible and openly discussed, using the metalanguage of genre-based instruction? First of all, in their assignments and discussions with students, faculty should answer these questions about the required texts, using the Rhetorical Planning Wheel (see Q10) as a guide:

- What is the assignment called? That is, what is its genre? If faculty use a general term like *essay* or *research paper*, what does *essay* mean in this particular classroom? Is there a more specific, descriptive term found in the discipline?
- What is the purpose for this assignment? Are students defining, answering a question, critiquing a reading or methodology, summarizing or paraphrasing sources, or

something else? That is, what rhetorical actions will students be taking?

- What sources or theories should be woven into this assignment? How many sources? Do the students search for them or are they provided?

- Is there an audience for the students' texts in addition to the instructor? What does this audience know? What does it value?

- What role(s) do the student writers take on in the text? Are the writers experts, explorers, new to the topic, for example?

- Is the context the classroom—or someplace else?

- How should the assigned text be structured? Is there a particular way that coherence is achieved, such as through the use of headings, in the required genre?

- What register should the paper be written in? What specialized vocabulary should the student be employing? Should the student make and defend claims or present information? Should they write impersonally or in the first person?

- What formatting conventions should be employed? APA headings, for example?

Particularly valuable for student understanding would be two or more outstanding examples of previous students' work in the same or a similar task. Faculty can prepare students to analyze these texts, asking what they notice. Or faculty can employ a "reading protocol" during which they themselves go through one or more of the exemplar texts and explain what the writers were doing—and why. Unfortunately, exemplar texts are not always available; or, on the other hand, faculty may believe that exploring exemplars will diminish the students' creativity. However, if they overcome these concerns, faculty may find that they receive much more successful responses to their assignments.

In order to discuss assignments in depth, faculty will need some of the metalanguage mentioned in this volume. Here are the terms that we have found to be particularly useful: moves in discourse (Q12), register (Q14), framing sentences (Q16, Q22), and passive/active voice (Q17).

# 39 How do I explain genre to an administrator?

At some point you may find yourself in the position of having to explain genre to colleagues, including administrators. Perhaps you need to convince them of the value of bringing genre into the classroom or rebuilding a curriculum around genres rather than modes (see Q5). Or you may need to justify a focus on genre or explain a learning outcome related to genre. Depending on the expertise and disciplinary background of the administrator, you might take different approaches.

If your goal is to describe what genre is, we suggest explaining mainly through examples, since those are tangible and usually relatable. Give examples of the many genres that we use to communicate in our personal and professional lives: wedding invitations, consumer reviews, letters of complaint, letters of recommendation, scholarship or fellowship application essays, research proposals, and so on. It can be useful to emphasize that there is no *one* way to write, which is what makes writing (and writing instruction) so difficult. Instead, students have to learn to analyze and use *many* different genres in and out of school. You might also help administrators relate to how they themselves have learned genres: through experience, support from more experienced people, examples and models of effective texts, and feedback from successful and failed attempts. Some genres—especially academic and professional genres—are difficult to learn because they vary across audiences and settings.

Many writing programs have an explicit mission of preparing students for writing in other contexts. Intensive English Programs and English for Academic Purposes programs prepare students for undergraduate and graduate degrees taught all or partly in English; first-year writing courses at universities often have the mission of readying students for writing tasks in future courses in their majors and other disciplines; one goal of many community colleges is to give students access to four-year universities. However, in all these situations, writing should not be reduced to preparation for "real" writing in some other course or place: It must be engaging and valued *in the present*. Students in language programs, undergraduate writing courses, and community colleges deserve to produce meaningful writing and wrestle with challenging genres *now*. Furthermore, it is rarely possible to predict with any accuracy, let alone teach, all the varied and often idiosyncratic genres students will encounter in their future degree programs and workplaces (e.g., Melzer, 2014). Therefore, reducing the purpose of writing courses to "preparation" is an ill-fated approach, which is an important point to emphasize to administrators.

Your colleagues, especially those with influence over curriculum and instruction, may also be interested to see examples of writing produced by students in genre-based classes. Many traditional curricula built around rhetorical modes, essays, and staid research papers frankly generate boring writing that students have little motivation to produce and teachers have little interest in reading. However, as we have emphasized throughout this book, genre-based writing assignments can be embedded in meaningful contexts so that students have a purpose for writing and an (imagined) audience for whom to write (Caplan & Johns, 2019; Eodice et al., 2017; Wardle, 2017). Those who have not taught a genre-based course may be surprised to see what your students can write when they are given contextualized everyday, academic, or professional genres to study and practice.

Once administrators understand that written communication generally occurs through genres, and that many genres are challenging to learn, they may be supportive of genre-based approaches to teaching writing. It can be helpful to explain that an additional goal of such instruction is to develop students' analytic skills so that they have strategies for analyzing and understanding unfamiliar genres inside and outside of the classroom. To use a common metaphor, we are not just giving students a fish, we are teaching them *how to* fish. Genre-based writing instruction may be more difficult than, say, teaching and writing five-paragraph essays, but it should equip students with the analytical skills for moving through many unknown writing situations in the future.

# 40 *What do I read next?*

Fortunately, there are many resources available to teachers interested in implementing genre pedagogies into their classes. The lists below provide a starting point.

## Practitioner-Focused Resources

Caplan, N. A., & Johns, A. M. (Eds.). (2019). *Changing practices for the L2 writing classroom: Moving beyond the five-paragraph essay.* University of Michigan Press.

    This collection of ten chapters explains how practitioners can move beyond the five-paragraph essay to genre-based instruction.

Cheng, A. (2018). *Genre and graduate-level research writing.* University of Michigan Press.

    Designed for graduate instructors, this accessible monograph contains suggestions for teaching materials and approaches applicable to all post-secondary levels.

Coffin, C., Curry, M. J., Goodman, S., Hewings, A., Lillis, T. M., & Swann, J. (2003). *Teaching academic writing: A toolkit for higher education.* Routledge.

    A very practical guide to writing instruction that clearly shows similarities and differences among common pedagogical and disciplinary genres.

Ferris, D. R., & Hedgecock, J. S. (2014). *Teaching L2 composition: Purpose, process, and practice.* (3rd ed.). Routledge.

    A popular textbook covering all facets of teaching writing, including discussion of genre-based instruction.

Hyland, K. (2004). *Genre and second language writing.* University of Michigan Press.

    A clear summary of the three major theoretical approaches to genre in L2 writing with practical examples and advice for teachers.

Hyon, S. (2018). *Introducing genre and English for Specific Purposes.* Routledge.

    Designed for teachers, this volume introduces the concept of genre and contains numerous practical tasks and examples for the classroom.

Johns, A. M. (1997). *Text, role, and context: Developing academic literacies.* Cambridge University Press.

This pedagogically focused monograph offers an early discussion, with tasks, on genre-based instruction and its roots.

Johns, A. M. (Ed.). (2002). *Genre in the classroom: Multiple perspectives.* Lawrence Erlbaum.

Chapters in this edited volume are motivated by one of the three major genre theories, demonstrating how these theories inform classroom instruction.

Melzer, D. (2014). *Assignments across the curriculum: A national study of college writing.* Utah State University Press.

This comprehensive study of more than 2,000 undergraduate writing assignments from 100 post-secondary institutions across the United States is a useful resource.

Nesi, H., & Gardner, S. (2012). *Genres across disciplines: Student writing in higher education.* Cambridge University Press.

Based on the British Academic Written English (BAWE, rhymes with *saw*) corpus, Nesi and Gardner identify thirteen *genre families* of undergraduate university writing. While the results are specific to British universities, many of the genres are common in other educational systems.

Paltridge, B. (1997). *Genre and the language learning classroom.* University of Michigan Press.

This small, practical book for teachers offers an overview of genre-based pedagogy for language teachers. Chapters address context, discourse, language, and assessment and include many sample activities.

Tardy, C. M. (2016). *Beyond convention: Genre innovation in academic writing.* University of Michigan Press.

This volume makes clear, through theory, research, and in-class tasks, how students can use genre to be motivated and creative as they explore both convention and variation.

Tardy, C. M. (2019). *Genre-based writing: What every ESL teacher needs to know.* University of Michigan Press.

Informed by research, this practical, short ebook is written for teachers new to genre pedagogy and includes numerous accessible activities and explanations for the classroom.

# Genre-Based Textbooks

Swales, J. M., & Feak, C. B. (2012). *Academic writing for graduate students: Essential tasks and skills* (3rd ed.). University of Michigan Press.

An excellent textbook for graduate students and researchers that helps writers produce several foundational genres, including summaries, syntheses, data commentaries, and empirical research papers. The volume includes explanations and activities for students, most of which are applicable to many academic levels.

Caplan, N. A., & Johns, A. M. (2022). *Essential actions for academic writing.* University of Michigan Press.

This genre-based textbook is aimed at novice undergraduate writers, including English learners and multilingual students. Students learn to use the key actions of academic writing (explain, summarize, synthesize, report and interpret data, argue, analyze, and respond) and apply them to pedagogical, everyday, professional, and disciplinary genres.


# Genre Theory

Bawarshi, A. S., & Reiff, M. J. (2010). *Genre: An introduction to history, theory, research, and pedagogy.* WAC Clearinghouse.

This open-source reference book offers a strong starting point for understanding a wide range of genre theories, with a particular focus on rhetorical genre studies.

Devitt, A. J. (2004). *Writing genres.* Southern Illinois University Press.

This book explores genre theory, including history, creativity, and literary genres. The final chapter offers a theoretically grounded proposal for teaching genre awareness to early undergraduate writers.

Rose, D., & Martin, J. R. (2012). *Learning to write, reading to learn: Genre, knowledge, and pedagogy in the Sydney School.* Equinox.

A clear introduction to key principles in the genre theory that emerged from Halliday's Systemic Functional Linguistics at the University of Sydney.

Schleppegrell, M. (2004). *The language of schooling.* Lawrence Erlbaum.

This book was one of the first to introduce Systemic Functional Linguistics in a clear and accessible way to North American audience. Although Schleppegrell's focus is on K-12 settings, the volume is highly relevant to writing in ESL and higher education.

Swales, J. M. (1990). *Genre analysis: English in academic and research settings.* Cambridge: Cambridge University Press.

This volume is the gold standard, the basis on which much of current genre theory and pedagogy is based. As is the case of most books about genre, this volume draws repeatedly from Swales's definitions and insights.

# References

Accurso K., Gebhard M., Harris G., & Schuetz J. (2021). Implications of genre pedagogy for refugee youth with limited or interrupted formal schooling. In D. S. Warriner (Ed.), *Refugee education across the lifespan* (pp. 57–78). Springer.

Artemeva N., & Myles D. N. (2015). Perceptions of prior genre knowledge: A case of incipient biliterate writers in the EAP classroom. In G. Down & N. Rulyova (Eds.), *Genre trajectories* (pp. 225–245). Palgrave Macmillan. https://doi.org/10.1057/97811 37505484_13

Bartholomae, D. (1985). Inventing the university. In M. Rose (Ed.), *When a writer can't write: Studies in writer's block and other composing process problems* (pp. 134–65). Guilford Press.

Bazerman, C. (1988). *Shaping written knowledge: The genre and activity of the experimental article in science.* University of Wisconsin Press.

Belcher, D. D. (2006). English for specific purposes: Teaching to perceived needs and imagined futures in worlds of work, study, and everyday life. *TESOL Quarterly, 40* (1), 133–156. https://doi.org/10.2307/40264514

Belcher, D. D. (2017). On becoming facilitators of multimodal composing and digital design. *Journal of Second Language Writing, 38,* 80–85. https://doi.org/10.1016/ j.jslw.2017.10.004

Biber, D., & Barbieri, F. (2007). Lexical bundles in university spoken and written registers. *English for Specific Purposes, 26,* 263–286. https://doi.org/10.1016/j.esp.2006.08.003

Blum, S. D. (Ed.). (2020). *Ungrading: Why rating students undermines learning.* West Virginia University Press.

Brisk, M. E. (2018). *Engaging students in academic literacies: Genre-based pedagogy for K-5 classrooms.* Routledge.

Brisk, M. E., & Schleppegrell, M. J. (2021). *Language in action: SFL theory across contexts.* Equinox.

Caplan, N. A. (2019). *Grammar choices for graduate and professional writers* (2nd ed). University of Michigan Press.

Caplan, N. A., & Farling, M. (2017). A dozen heads are better than one: Collaborative writing in genre-based pedagogy. *TESOL Journal, 8* (3), 564–581. https://doi.org/ 10.1002/tesj.287

Caplan, N. A., & Johns, A. M. (Eds.). (2019). *Changing practices for the L2 writing classroom: Moving beyond the five-paragraph essay.* University of Michigan Press.

Caplan, N. A., & Johns, A. M. (2022). *Essential actions for academic writing.* University of Michigan Press.

Carson, A. D. (2017). *Owning my masters: Rhetorics of rhymes & revolutions* [Doctoral dissertation]. Retrieved from *All Dissertations.* (1885).

Charles, M. (2014). Getting the corpus habit: EAP students' long-term use of personal corpora. *English for Specific Purposes, 35,* 30–40. https://doi.org/10.1016/j.esp.2013.11.004

Cheng, A. (2007). Transferring generic features and recontextualizing genre awareness: Understanding writing performance in the ESP genre-based literacy framework. *Journal of Second Language Writing, 26,* 287–307. https://doi.org/10.1016/j.esp.2006.12.002

Cheng, A. (2018). *Genre and graduate-level research writing.* University of Michigan Press.

Cisneros, S. (1984). *The house on mango street.* Vintage.

Colorado Department of Education. (n.d.). *Reflective questions for students.* https://www.cde.state.co.us/standardsandinstruction/es-student-reflections-mc

Connor, U. M., & Ene, E. (2019). Does everyone write the five-paragraph essay? In N. A. Caplan & A. M. Johns (Eds.), *Changing practices for the L2 writing classroom: Moving beyond the five-paragraph essay* (pp. 42–63). University of Michigan Press.

Coxhead, A. (2000). A new academic word list. *TESOL Quarterly, 34*(2), 213–238. https://doi.org/10.2307/3587951

de Oliveira, L. C., & Iddings, J. (Eds.). (2014). *Genre pedagogy across the curriculum: Theory and application in U.S. classrooms and contexts.* Equinox.

de Oliveira, L. C., Jones, L., & Smith, S. L. (2020). Interactional scaffolding in a first-grade classroom through the teaching–learning cycle. *International Journal of Bilingual Education and Bilingualism.* https://doi.org/10.1080/13670050.2020.1798867

Derish, P. A., & Annesley, T. M. (2010). If an IRDAM journal is what you choose, then sequential results are what you use. *Clinical Chemistry, 56,* 1226–1228. https://doi.org/10.1373/clinchem.2010.150961

Devitt, A. J. (2009). Teaching critical genre awareness. In C. Bazerman, A. Bonini, & D. Figueiredo (Eds.), *Genre in a changing world: Perspectives on writing* (pp. 337–351). The WAC Clearinghouse; Parlor Press. https://wac.colostate.edu/books/perspectives/genre/

Devitt, A. J., Bawarshi, A., & Reiff, M. J. (2004). *Scenes of writing: Strategies for composing with genres.* Pearson Longman.

Dryer, D. B. (2015). "The fact that I could write about it made me think it was real": An interview with Carolyn R. Miller. *Composition Forum, 31*. https://compositionforum. com/issue/31/carolyn-miller-interview.php

Dudley-Evans, T., & St. John, M. (1998). *Developments in English for Specific Purposes.* Cambridge University Press.

Eid, C., & Johns, A. M. (2010). *Teachers' guide to English language courses: 2010–2015.* Antonine University Press.

Elbow, P. (1997). Grading student writing: Making it simpler, fairer, clearer. *New Directions for Teaching & Learning, 69*, 127–140. https://doi.org/10.1002/tl.6911

Elola, I., & Oskoz, A. (2017). Writing with 21st century social tools in the L2 classroom: New literacies, genres, and writing practices. *Journal of Second Language Writing, 36*, 52–60. http://dx.doi.org/10.1016/j.jslw.2017.04.002

Eodice, M., Geller, A. E., & Lerner, N. (2017). *Learning, teaching and writing in higher education.* Utah State University Press.

Feak, C. B., & Swales, J. M. (2009). *Telling a research story: Writing a literature review.* University of Michigan Press.

Feez, S. (1998). *Text-based syllabus design.* National Centre for English Language Teaching and Research.

Ferris, D. (2011). *Treatment of error in second language student writing.* University of Michigan Press.

Ferris, D., & Hayes, H. (2019). Transferable principles and practices in undergraduate writing. In N. A. Caplan & A. M. Johns (Eds.), *Changing practices for the L2 writing classroom: Moving beyond the five-paragraph essay* (pp. 116–132). University of Michigan Press.

Flowerdew, L. (2013). Needs analysis and curriculum development in ESP. In B. Paltridge & S. Starfield (eds.). *The handbook of English for specific purposes* (pp. 325–46). Wiley-Blackwell.

Forman, J., & Rymer, J. (1999). The genre system of the Harvard case method. *Journal of Business and Technical Communication, 13*(4), 373–400. https://doi.org/10.1177/105 065199901300401

Freedman, A. (1993). Show and tell? The role of explicit teaching in the learning of new genres. *Research in the Teaching of English, 27*(3), 222–251.

Gentil, G. (2011). A biliteracy literacy agenda for genre research. *Journal of Second Language Writing, 20*, 6–23. https://doi.org/10.1016/j.jslw.2010.12.006

Hafner, C. A. (2015). Remix culture and English language teaching: The expression of learner voice in digital multimodal compositions. *TESOL Quarterly, 49*, 486–509. http:// dx.doi.org/10.1002/tesq.238.

Halliday, M. A. K. (1993). Towards a language-based theory of learning. *Linguistics and Education*, 5(2), 93–116. https://doi.org/10.1016/0898-5898(93)90026-7

Halliday, M. A. K., & Hasan, R. (1976). *Cohesion in English*. Longman.

Harman, R. M., & Burke, K. J. (2020). *Culturally sustaining system functional linguistics praxis*. Routledge.

Harris, A. (2010). *Cross-marked: Sudanese-Australian young women talk education* [Unpublished doctoral dissertation]. Victoria University, Melbourne, Australia.

Hinds, J. (1987). Teacher vs. writer-responsibility: A new typology. In U. Connor & R. B.Kaplan (Eds.), *Writing across languages: Analyses of L2 texts* (pp. 141–52). Addison Wesley.

Hinkel, E. (2002). *Second language writers' text: Linguistic and rhetorical features*. Lawrence Erlbaum.

Humphrey, S., & Macnaught, L. (2016). Functional language instruction and the writing growth of English language learners in the middle years. *TESOL Quarterly*, 50(4), 792–816. https://doi.org/10.1002/tesq.247

Hyland, K. (2004). *Genre and second language writing*. University of Michigan Press.

Hyland, K. (2005). Stance and engagement: A model of interaction in academic discourse. *Discourse Processes*, 7(2), 173–92. https://doi.org/10.1177%2F146144560 5050365

Hyland, K. (2008). As can be seen: Lexical bundles and disciplinary variation. *English for Specific Purposes*, 27, 4–21. https://doi.org/10.1016/j.esp.2007.06.001

Hyland, K. (2011). The presentation of self in scholarly life: Identity and marginalization in academic homepages. *English for Specific Purposes*, 30, 286–297. https://doi.org/10.1016/j.esp.2011.04.004

Hyland, K., & Tse, P. (2007). Is there an "academic vocabulary"? *TESOL Quarterly*, 41, 235–53. https://doi.org/10.1002/j.1545-7249.2007.tb00058.x

Hyland, K., & Tse, P. (2012). "She has received many honours": Identity construction in article bio statements. *Journal of English for Academic Purposes*, 11, 155–165. https://doi.org/10.1016/j.jeap.2012.01.001

Hyon. S. (2018). *Introducing genre and English for Specific Purposes*. New York: Routledge.

Inoue, A. (2014). A grade-less writing course that focuses on labor and assessing. In D. Coxwell-Teague & R. F. Lunsford (Eds.), *First-year composition: From theory to practice* (pp. 71–110). Parlor Press.

Johns, A. M. (1993). Written argumentation for real audiences: Suggestions for teacher research and classroom practice. *TESOL Quarterly*, 27, 75–90. https://doi.org/10.2307/3586952

Johns, A. M. (1997). *Text, role, and context: Developing academic literacies.* Cambridge University Press.

Johns, A. M. (2002a). Destabilizing and enriching novice students' genre theories. In A. M. Johns (Ed.), *Genre in the classroom: Multiple perspectives* (pp. 237–48). Lawrence Erlbaum Associates.

Johns, A. M. (Ed.). (2002b). *Genre in the classroom: Multiple perspectives.* Lawrence Erlbaum Associates.

Johns, A. M. (2015). Moving on from *Genre Analysis*: An update and tasks for the transitional student. *Journal of English for Academic Purposes, 19,* 113–124. https://doi.org/10.1016/j.jeap.2015.04.005

Johns, A. M. (2019). Writing in the interstices: Assisting novice undergraduates in analyzing authentic writing tasks. In N. A. Caplan & A. M. Johns (Eds.), *Changing practices for the L2 writing classroom: Moving beyond the five-paragraph essay* (pp. 133–148). University of Michigan Press.

Johns, A. M., & Makalela, L. (2011). Needs analysis, critical ethnography, and context: Perspectives from the client—and the consultant. In D. Belcher, A. M. Johns, & B. Paltridge (Eds.), *New directions in English for Specific Purposes research* (pp. 197–221). University of Michigan Press.

Liardét, C. L., & Black, S. (2019). "So and so" says, states and argues: A corpus-assisted engagement analysis of reporting verbs. *Journal of Second Language Writing, 44,* 37–50. https://doi.org/10.1016/j.jslw.2019.02.001

Long, M. H. (Ed.). (2005). *Second language needs analysis.* Cambridge University Press.

Lunsford, A., & Ruszkiewicz, J. J. (2012). *Everything's an argument* (6th ed.). Bedford/St. Martins.

Luzón, M.-J., & Pérez-Llantada, C. (2019). Connecting traditional and new genres: Trends and emerging themes. In C. Pérez-Llantada & M.-J. Luzón (Eds.), *Science communication on the internet: Old genres meet new genres* (pp. 1–18). Johns Benjamins.

Maley, A., & Peachey, N. (Eds.). (2015). *Creativity in the English language classroom.* British Council. https://www.teachingenglish.org.uk/article/creativity-english-language-classroom

Mapes, A. C., Jacobson, B., LaMance, R., & Vogel, S. (2020). Troublesome knowledge: A study of GTA ambivalence with genre-informed pedagogy. *Writing Program Administration, 43*(2), 66–88.

Martin, J. R. (2009). Genre and language learning: A social semiotic perspective. *Linguistics and Education, 20*(1), 10–21. https://doi.org/10.1016/j.linged.2009.01.003

Martin, J., & White, P. (2005). *The language of evaluation: Appraisal in English.* Palgrave Macmillan. https://doi.org/10.1057/9780230511910

McCulloch, G. (2019). *Because Internet: Understanding the new rules of language.* Riverhead Books.

Melzer, D. (2014). *Assignments across the curriculum: A national study of college writing.* Utah State University Press.

Miller, C. R. (1984). Genre as social action. *Quarterly Journal of Speech, 70*, 151–67. https://doi.org/10.1080/00335638409383686

Miller, R. T., Mitchel, T. D., & Pessoa, S. (2016). Impact of source texts and prompts on students' genre uptake. *Journal of Second Language Writing, 31*, 11–24. https://doi.org/10.1016/j.jslw.2016.01.001

Negretti, R., & McGrath, L. (2018). Scaffolding genre knowledge and metacognition: Insights from an L2 doctoral research writing course. *Journal of Second Language Writing, 40*, 12–31. https://doi.org/10.1016/j.jslw.2017.12.002

Nesi, H., & Gardner, S. (2012). *Genres across the disciplines: Student writing in higher education.* Cambridge University Press.

Ortmeier-Hooper, C. (2017). *Writing across language and culture: Inclusive strategies for working with ELL writers in the ELL classroom.* NCTE Press.

Ortmeier-Hooper, C. (2019). Rethinking the five-paragraph essay as a scaffold in secondary school. In N. A. Caplan & A. M. Johns (Eds.), *Changing practices for the L2 writing classroom: Moving beyond the five-paragraph essay* (pp. 89–115). University of Michigan Press.

Palese, E. (2021). *Prompting students to write: Designing and using second language writing assessment prompts* [Unpublished doctoral dissertation]. University of Arizona.

Paré, A. (2002). Genre and identity: Individuals, institutions, and ideology. In R. Coe, L. Lingard, & T. Teslenko (Eds.), *The rhetoric and ideology of genre* (pp. 57–71). Hampton Press.

Paré, A., Starke-Meyerring, D., & McAlpine, L. (2017). The dissertation as multi-genre: Many readers, many readings. In C. Bazerman, A. Bonini, & D. Figueiredo (Eds.), *Genre in a changing world* (pp. 183–197). WAC Clearing House and Parlor Press. https://wac.colostate.edu/BOOKS/GENRE/genre.pdf#page=195

Pessoa, S., & Mitchell, T. D. (2019). Preparing students to write in the disciplines. In N. A. Caplan & A. M. Johns (Eds.), *Changing practices for the L2 writing classroom: Moving beyond the five-paragraph essay* (pp. 150–177). University of Michigan Press.

Phillips, R., & Kara, H. (2021). *Creative writing for social research: A practical guide.* Policy Press.

Pintrich, Paul R. (2002). The role of metacognitive knowledge in learning, teaching, and assessing. *Theory into Practice, 41*(4), 219–225.

Polio, C. (2019). Keeping the language in second language writing classes. *Journal of Second Language Writing*, *46*, 100675. https://doi.org/10.1016/j.jslw.2019.100675

Qi, X. & Liu, L. (2007). Differences between reader/writer responsible languages reflected in EFL learners' writing. *Intercultural Communication Studies, 3*, 148–159.

Ravelli, L., Paltridge, B., & Starfield, S. (Eds.). (2014). *Doctoral writing in the creative and performing arts*. Libri Publishing.

Reiff, M. J., & Bawarshi, A. (2011). Tracing discursive resources: How students use prior genre knowledge to negotiate new writing contexts in first-year composition. *Written Communication, 28*(3), 312–337. https://doi.org/10.1177%2F0741088311410183

Rose, D., & Martin, J. R. (2012). *Learning to write, reading to learn: Genre, knowledge and pedagogy in the Sydney School*. Equinox.

Rothery, J. (1996). Making changes: Developing an educational linguistics. In R. Hasan & G. Williams (Eds.), *Literacy in society* (pp. 86–123). Longman.

Rounsaville, A., Goldberg, R., & Bawarsh, A. (2008). From incomes to outcomes: FYW students' prior knowledge, metacognition, and the question of transfer. *WPA: Writing Program Administration, 32*(1), 97–112.

Rozycki, W., & Johnson, N. H. (2013). Non-canonical grammar in Best Paper award winners in engineering. *English for Specific Purposes, 32*(3), 157–169. doi:10.1016/j.esp.2013.04.002

Samraj, B. (2004). Discourse features of the student-produced academic research paper: Variations across disciplinary courses. *Journal of English for Academic Purposes, 3*(1), 5–22. https://doi.org/10.1016/S1475-1585(03)00053-5

Samraj, B. (2013). Form and function of citations in discussion sections of master's theses and research articles. *Journal of English for Academic Purposes, 12*, 299–310.

Scherff, L., & Piazza, C. (2005). The more things change, the more they stay the same: A survey of high school students' writing experiences. *Research in the Teaching of English, 39*(3), 271–305.

Schleppegrell, M. J. (2004). *The language of schooling: A functional linguistics perspective*. Lawrence Erlbaum.

Schryer, C. F. (1993). Records as genre. *Written Communication, 10*, 200–234. https://doi.org/10.1177%2F0741088393010002003

Simpson-Vlach, R., & Ellis, N. C. (2010). An academic formulas list: New methods in phraseology research. *Applied Linguistics, 31*, 487–512. https://doi.org/10.1093/applin/amp058

Sommer-Farias, B. (2020). *"This is helping me with writing in all languages": Developing genre knowledge across languages in a foreign language course* (Publication No. 27996128) [Doctoral dissertation, University of Arizona]. ProQuest Dissertations Publishing.

Sousanis, N. (2015). *Unflattening: A dissertation in comics from reimagined scholarship and academic writing* [Unpublished doctoral dissertation, Columbia University].

Spack, R. (1997). The acquisition of academic literacy in a second language: A longitudinal case study. *Written Communication, 14*(3), 3–62. https://doi.org/10.1177%2F07410883 97014001001

Swain, M., & Lapkin, S. (2002). Talking it through: Two French immersion learners' response to reformulation. *International Journal of Educational Research, 37*(3–4), 285–304. https://doi.org/10.1016/S0883-0355(03)00006-5

Swales, J. M. (1990). *Genre analysis: English in academic and research settings.* Cambridge University Press.

Swales, J. M. (1996). Occluded genres in the academy: The case of the submission letter. In E. Ventola & A. Mauranen (Eds.), *Academic writing: Intercultural and textual issues* (pp. 45–58). John Benjamins.

Swales, J. M. (2004). *Research genres: Explorations and applications.* Cambridge University Press.

Swales, J. M. (2009). When there is no perfect text: Approaches to the EAP practitioner's dilemma. *Journal of English for Academic Purposes, 8,* 5–13.

Swales, J. M., & Feak, C. B. (2012). *Academic writing for graduate students: Essential tasks and skills* (3rd ed.). University of Michigan Press.

Tardy, C. M. (2005). Expressions of disciplinarity and individuality in a multimodal genre. *Computers and Composition, 27*(3), 319–336.

Tardy, C. M. (2009). *Building genre knowledge.* Parlor Press.

Tardy, C. M. (2016). *Beyond convention: Genre innovation in academic writing.* University of Michigan Press.

Tardy, C. M. (2019a). *Genre-based writing: What every ESL teacher needs to know.* University of Michigan Press.

Tardy, C. M. (2019b). Is the five-paragraph essay a genre? In N. A. Caplan & A. M. Johns (Eds.), *Changing practices for the L2 writing classroom: Moving beyond the five-paragraph essay* (pp. 24–41). University of Michigan Press.

Tardy, C. M., Buck, R. H., Jacobson, B., LaMance, R., Pawloski, M., Slinkard, J., & Vogel, S. (2022). "It's complicated and nuanced": Teaching genre awareness in English for general academic purposes. *Journal of English for Academic Purposes, 57,* 101117.

Tardy, C. M., Sommer-Farias, B., & Gevers, J. (2020). Teaching and researching genre knowledge: Toward an enhanced theoretical framework. *Written Communication, 37*(3), 287–321. https://doi.org/10.1177%2F0741088320916554

Tardy, C. M., & Swales, J. M. (2014). Genre analysis. In A. Barron & K. P. Schneider (Eds.), *Pragmatics of discourse* (pp. 165–187). Berlin: Mouton de Gruyter.

Tarone, E., Dwyer, S., Gillette, S., & Icke, V. (1981). On the use of the passive in two astrophysics journal papers. *The ESP Journal, 1,* 123–140. https://doi.org/10.1016/0272-2380(81)90004-4

Wardle, E. (2017). You can learn to write in general. In C. E. Ball & D. M. Loewe (Eds.), *Bad ideas about writing* (pp. 30–33). West Virginia University Libraries. http://textbooks.lib.wvu.edu

Wette, R. (2017). Using mind maps to reveal and develop genre knowledge in a graduate writing course. *Journal of Second Language Writing, 38,* 58–71. https://doi.org/10.1016/j.jslw.2017.09.005

WIDA. (2020). *WIDA English language development standards framework, 2020 edition: Kindergarten–grade 12.* Board of Regents of the University of Wisconsin System. https://wida.wisc.edu/sites/default/files/resource/WIDA-ELD-Standards-Framework-2020.pdf

Wingate, U. (2012). "Argument!" helping students understand what essay writing is about. *Journal of English for Academic Purposes, 11*(2), 145–154. https://doi.org/10.1016/j.jeap.2011.11.001

Worden, D. (2019). Developing L2 writing teachers' pedagogical content knowledge of genre through the unfamiliar genre project. *Journal of Second Language Writing, 46,* 1–12.

Yancey, K., Robertson, L., & Taczak, K. (2015). *Writing across contexts: Transfer, composition, and site of writing.* Utah State University Press.

Yasuda, S. (2011). Genre-based tasks in foreign language writing: Developing writers' genre awareness, linguistic knowledge, and writing competence. *Journal of Second Language Writing, 20*(2), 111–133. https://doi.org/10.1016/j.jslw.2011.03.001